Turn It Up!

Music in Poetry from Jazz to Hip-Hop

D1295767

TURN IT UP!

MUSIC IN POETRY
FROM JAZZ TO HIP-HOP

EDITED BY
STEPHEN CRAMER

Sundog Poetry Center & Green Writers Press

Printed in the United States

10 9 8 7 6 5 4 3 2 1

Green Writers Press is a Vermont-based publisher whose mission is to spread a message of hope and renewal through the words and images we publish. Throughout we will adhere to our commitment to preserving and protecting the natural resources of the earth. To that end, a percentage of our proceeds will be donated to environmental activist groups. Green Writers Press gratefully acknowledges support from individual donors, friends, and readers to help support the environment and our publishing initiative.

Giving Voice to Writers & Artists Who Will Make the World a Better Place
Green Writers Press | West Brattleboro, Vermont
www.greenwriterspress.com

Sundog Poetry Center, Inc.
www.sundogpoetry.org

ISBN: 978-1-950584-32-1

Cover by Michael J. Balzano

THE PAPER USED IN THIS PUBLICATION IS PRODUCED BY MILLS COMMITTED
TO RESPONSIBLE AND SUSTAINABLE FORESTRY PRACTICES.

*For Holly Brevent and Val Rohy, who urged me
to create the course that created this book.*

There's music in the sighing of a reed;
   There's music in the gushing of a rill;
      There's music in all things, if men had ears:
        Their earth is but an echo of the spheres.

—Lord Byron, from *Don Juan*

·

Well, back to the back to the beat, y'all,
   Down with the sound so sweet, y'all.
      Just how fresh can ya get, y'all?
        Those that are blessed say *yes y'all!*

—Beastie Boys, from *Live at P.J.'s*

Contents

Singing Hellhounds: Poems about Blues, Rock, & Pop

Yes Yes, Y'all: Poems about Hip-Hop

Introduction

THE NOW FAMOUS QUOTE has been attributed to everyone from Steve Martin to Frank Zappa to Thelonious Monk: *writing about music is like dancing about architecture.* It just can't be done, some say. The two arts are irreconcilable, some say. How can one pin down an invisible craft like music with the more absolute definitions of language? Well, you're holding in your hands proof that it can be done, and done in style. The poets in *Turn It Up!* have responded to everyone from Louis Armstrong to the Rolling Stones to Public Enemy, and their work is all the richer for the exchange.

David Jauss writes, "If we want to understand the poetry of our time fully, then we must try to understand why it so often turns to jazz for inspiration." I would extend this sentiment to include music in general. Why does David Wojahn turn to Richie Valens in his work? Why does Adrian Matejka turn to Q-Tip? One easy answer is: nostalgia. Poets want to revisit their youth and the first time music shoved them out onto a dance floor, or made them sing in the shower, or gave them the permission to ask the right girl or boy out. But the connection obviously goes deeper than that. Another part of what makes music so captivating and memorable to poets is that both arts place such emphasis on rhythm.

Rhythm is a mysterious tool. As Robert Hass writes, it "has direct access to the unconscious . . . it can hypnotize us, enter our bodies and make us move." This gives it an immense power over us. We, as a species, instinctively listen for rhythms, even when we don't realize it. Imagine camping in the woods at night. Everything is just fine as the crickets keep chirping their two-beat song. But if their music is interrupted by the snapping of a twig, and all the crickets simultaneously hush up, every last one of us would sit up, rigid, and look around. Something in our environment has changed. Our hunter/gatherer forebears felt this instinct keenly, but we carry the same impulse with us into the 21st century.

We listen for the rhythm of the train coming down the tracks, suggesting that the flow of people on the platform is about to drastically change. At intersections we listen to the rhythm of the chirping *walk* sign, anticipating its shift into silence, suggesting we better get our hides across the street to safety. The rhythms of the world, both rural and urban, call to us. Without even asking our permission, the music and poetry that make use of these rhythms can hitch a ride on our heartbeats where they can console us, comfort us, and even sustain us. Doctors help us to live, but they don't give us what we live *for*. That task is up to Dr. John and Dr. Dre.

Every generation takes the material that they're given and shapes it, as it has shaped them. Shakespeare and Whitman wrote brilliantly, but neither could have written a poem about Charlie Parker or Miles Davis to save his life. William Wordsworth is a giant of literature, but he couldn't have written a poem about Nirvana or the Beastie Boys; he couldn't have written a poem with the distinct inflection, diction, and syntax that hip-hop has so recently delivered to our doorsteps. The style of any period needs to be challenged or else the succeeding period's work will grow dry and crumble away. It's hard to argue against the statement that each generation's music has, decade by decade, injected a new vitality into American poetry.

A few words about this anthology. Though there have been a number of collections of poetry about music (*The Jazz Poetry Anthology* and *The Second Set*, edited by Sascha Feinstein and Yusef Komunyakaa, *Sweet Nothings: An Anthology of Rock and Roll in American Poetry*, edited by Jim Elledge, and *The BreakBeat Poets: New American Poetry in the Age of Hip-Hop*, edited by Kevin Coval, Quraysh Ali Lansana, and Nate Marshall come to mind as some of the strongest), none have crossed all the musical genres. *Turn It Up!* allows the reader to see the progression of poems about different styles of music, and how they may overlap, and how the diction and syntax and subject matter changes over time.

The work that is eligible for this anthology is that which responds to the music or musicians of the 20th and 21st centuries, which is to say, thousands upon thousands of poems. I think it's evident that this anthology is far from complete. Any time you narrow down an entire genre to 40 or so selections apiece, a lot of important work is going to be left by the wayside. This book skips, for instance, some of the earlier work about jazz, which essentially misunderstand the music (some of the work of Vachel Lindsay comes to mind, and even that of greats like William Carlos Williams). It skips much of the Beat generation's work (giants like Kenneth Patchen and Kenneth Rexroth, for instance). And by necessity it skips plenty of contemporary poetry that is being revealed daily in all the best journals. This book is like a single drop of salt water that stands for the ocean; you can get the general taste of it, but it's up to you to imagine what it's like to be far out at sea, buffeted by the waves, hovering over the deep. Maybe the book will inspire you to read more. Bring a sturdy raft.

"If you don't live it," Charlie Parker said, "it won't come out your horn." As their words make evident, many of these poets have lived with and *through* (if not *because of*) the music, whether it be snaking from a pair of headphones, blasting from a boom box, roaring from a car radio with the windows rolled down, or easing from the living room stereo. These poets have lived through these musicians and their songs, and they have created a new music out of their exchange with them. Let us lend them our ears.

—S.C.

A Shower of Golden Eighth Notes:

Poems about Jazz

Archangel

for Chet Baker

AI

You stepped through
the Van Gogh blue curtain
into my dream.
That day in Paris,
we sat at the outdoor café for hours.
I had high breasts
and my dress was cut low.
You leaned close to me, so close;
yet, did not touch.
"I don't need to," you said, "it's the dope,
it's the rush
so much better than lust.
Hush, take a deep breath
and you'll just go to sleep like I did."
I knew you were hustling me,
that underneath the hipster philosophy
lay the same old Chet out to score.
Still, I lent you money, still I followed you
to the pissoir,
where Lucien gave you "le fix."
Shaking his head, he pocketed the money and said,
"I heard you were dead,"
and you answered, "I am."
You said when you slammed into the pavement,
Amsterdam shook, then settled back into apathy,
the way we all do, when we are through
with the foolishness of living.

You ended up sharing your works with a whore
who waited outside the pissoir door,
your generosity as pathetic
as it was predictable.
You wanted sainthood like everybody else.
Instead, you earned the wings
that were too late to save you,
but not too late to raise you
up to junkie heaven.
Later, we stood on the steps of Notre Dame.
You were calm, as you pointed to the bell tower.
You said you saw Quasimodo up there,
holding Esmerelda over the edge
by her hair,
but all I saw staring down were the gargoyles
who'd found peace,
because it meant nothing to them.
"I see," I lied, to please you,
but you knew, and you blew me a kiss.
You wished me "bonne chance,"
then you eased into flight,
as the cool, jazzy, starry night
opened its arms to retrieve you.

Le sporting-club de Monte Carlo

for Lena Horne

JAMES BALDWIN

The lady is a tramp
    a camp
    a lamp

The lady is a sight
    a might
    a light
the lady devastated
an alley or two
reverberated through the valley
which leads to me, and you

the lady is the apple
of God's eye:
He's cool enough about it
but He tends to strut a little
when she passes by

the lady is a wonder
daughter of the thunder
smashing cages
legislating rages
with the voice of ages
singing us through.

AM/TRAK

Amiri Baraka

1

Trane,
Trane,
History Love Scream Oh
Trane, Oh
Trane, Oh
Scream History Love
Trane

2

Begin on by a Philly night club
or the basement of a cullut chuhch
walk the bars my man for pay
honk the night lust of money
oh
blow—
scream history love
Rabbit, Cleanhead, Diz
Big Maybelle, Trees in the shining night forest

Oh
blow
love, history

Alcohol we submit to thee
3x's consume our lives
our livers quiver under yr poison hits

eyes roll back in stupidness
The navy, the lord, niggers,
the streets
all converge a shitty symphony
of screams
  to come
  dazzled invective
Honk Honk Honk, "I am here
to love
it." Let me be fire-mystery
air feeder beauty"

Honk
Oh
scream—Miles
comes.

3

Hip band alright
sum up life in the slick
street part of the
world, oh,
blow,
if you cd
nigger
man

Miles wd stand back and negative check
oh, he dug him—Trane
But Trane clawed at the limits of cool
slandered sanity
with his tryin to be born
raging
shit

Oh
blow,
     yeh go do it
     honk, scream
     uhuh yeh—history
          love
          blue clipped moments
          of intense feeling.

"Trane you blows too long."
Screaming niggers drop out yr solos
Bohemian nights, the "heavyweight champ"
smacked him
in the face
his eyes sagged like a spent
dick, hot vowels escaped the metal clone of his soul
fucking saxophone
tell us shit tell us tell us!

4

There was nothing left to do but
be where monk cd find him
that crazy
mother fucker
     duh duh-duh duh-duh duh
     duh duh
     duh duh-duh duh-duh duh
     duh duh
     duh Duuuuuuuhhhhhh
Can you play this shit? (Life asks
Come by and listen

& at the 5 Spot Bach, Mulatto ass Beethoven
& even Duke, who had given America its hip tongue
checked
checked
Trane stood and dug
Crazy monk's shit
Street gospel intellectual mystical survival codes
Intellectual street gospel funk modes
Tink a ling put downs of dumb shit
pink pink a cool bam groove note air breath
a why I'm here
a why I aint
& who is you-ha-you-ha-you-ha

Monk's shit
Blue Cooper 5 Spot
was the world busting
on piano bass drums & tenor

This was Coltrane's College. A Ph motherfuckin d
sitting at the feet, elbows
& funny grin
Of Master T Sphere
too cool to be a genius
he was instead
Thelonious
with Comrades Shadow
on tubs, lyric Wilbur
who hipped us to electric futures
& the monster with the horn.

5

From the endless sessions
money lord hovers oer us

capitalism beats our ass
dope & juice wont change it
Trane, blow, oh scream
yeh, anyway.

There then came down in the ugly streets of us
inside the head & tongue
of us
a man
black blower of the now
The vectors from all sources—slavery, renaissance
bop charlie parker,
nigger absolute super-sane screams against reality
course through him
AS SOUND!
 "Yes, it says
this is now in you screaming
recognize the truth
recognize reality
& even check me (Trane)
who blows it

Yes it says
Yes &
Yes again   Convulsive multi orgasmic
              Art
              Protest

& finally, brother, you took you were
   (are we gathered to dig this?
   electric wind find us finally
   on red records of the history of ourselves)

The cadre came together
the inimitable 4 who blew the pulse of then, exact
The flame the confusion the love of

whatever the fuck there was
    to love
Yes it says
blow, oh honk-scream (bahhhhhh—wheeeeeee)

(If Don Lee thinks I am imitating him in this poem,
this is only payback for his imitating me—we
are brothers, even if he is a backward cultural nationalist
motherfucker—Hey man only socialism brought by
revolution
can win)
        Trane was the spirit of the 60's
        He was Malcolm X in New Super Bop Fire
        Baaahhhhh
        Wheeeeeee. . . . Black Art!!!
Love
History
  On The Bar Tops of Philly
in the Monkish College of Express
in the cool Grottoes of Miles Davis Funnytimery
Be
Be
Be reality
Be reality alive in motion in flame to change (You Knew It!)
                       to change!!
        (All you reactionaries listening
        Fuck you, Kill you
        get outta here!!!)

Jimmy Garrison, bass, McCoy Tyner, piano, Captain Marvel
Elvin
on drums, the number itself—the precise saying
all of it in it afire talking saying being doing meaning
Meditations,
Expressions
A Love Supreme

(I lay in solitary confinement, July 67
Tanks rolling thru Newark
& whistled all I knew of Trane
my knowledge heartbeat
& he was *dead*
they
said.

And yet last night I played *Meditations*
& it told me what to do
Live, you crazy mother
fucker!
Live!
  & organize
  yr shit
  as rightly
  burning!

Off Minor

Adrea Bogle

Layered in maroons, intermingled, uncleaving,
Blacktail Butte slopes to the Snake River
shaving grains. They say at Washakie
in '58, "Shunk" Dobbs carved three feet

into his cell with a fork's prong. That year
you & I raced from stinging nettle to limestone:
your mouth to my hip, our skin prickled in sweaty
irritation, my shoulder blades in a gravel bed . . .

The desert's arch slides from symmetry
into soiled pebbles a child might find among
Shanty's ponderosa & keep for the fit
between index finger & thumb. Rubbed for luck.

When Dobbs hit a spring, he flooded the block.
Two weeks in the hole, but that night they slept
heavy & guarded on the ground: Orion
& fallen apples sweetening to cider.

Have I told you about the woman whose weight
made her pull shirts over her knees
until eight kids lay on her, soothed by folds
all their own, or the baker kneading dough

while his foot pulsed beneath the counter
like Monk at his piano? The root
of this has everything to do with jazz
or molding clay, both hands in sync,

leaning to the center as the lip balances
with the finality of time & pressure.

but, ruby my dear

WANDA COLEMAN

he hikes those narrow chords one more time
to a dingy walkup on the outskirts of ecstasy
he knows every note of her
down to that maddening musky treble
from between her dusky thighs
even as he raps twice to let her know
he means business
and hears her singeful "who's there?"
as she unlocks the double bass count
he's gonna put hurt on her
he's gonna love her like winter loves snow
he's gonna make her
beyond that scratchy 78 whining dreary days and
whiskey nights
between that too sweet smoke andante
beyond that hunger for impossible freedom
to the heart of melody
where they will go to steam
in the jazzified mystical sanctity
of discordant fusion

scaling

Man Listening to Disc

BILLY COLLINS

This is not bad—
ambling along 44th Street
with Sonny Rollins for company,
his music flowing through the soft calipers
of these earphones,

as if he were right beside me
on this clear day in March,
the pavement sparkling with sunlight,
pigeons fluttering off the curb,
nodding over a profusion of bread crumbs.

In fact, I would say
my delight at being suffused
with phrases from his saxophone—
some like honey, some like vinegar—
is surpassed only by my gratitude

to Tommy Potter for taking the time
to join us on this breezy afternoon
with his most unwieldy bass
and to the esteemed Arthur Taylor
who is somehow managing to navigate

this crowd with his cumbersome drums.
And I bow deeply to Thelonious Monk
for figuring out a way
to motorize—or whatever—his huge piano
so he could be with us today.

This music is loud yet so confidential.
I cannot help feeling even more

like the center of the universe
than usual as I walk along to a rapid
little version of "The Way You Look Tonight,"

and all I can say to my fellow pedestrians,
to the woman in the white sweater,
the man in the tan raincoat and the heavy glasses,
who mistake themselves for the center of the universe—
all I can say is watch your step,

because the five of us, instruments and all,
are about to angle over
to the south side of the street
and then, in our own tightly knit way,
turn the corner at Sixth Avenue.

And if any of you are curious
about where this aggregation,
this whole battery-powered crew,
is headed, let us just say
that the real center of the universe,

the only true point of view,
is full of hope that he,
the hub of the cosmos
with his hair blown sideways,
will eventually make it all the way downtown.

Rose Solitude

for Duke Ellington

JAYNE CORTEZ

I am essence of Rose Solitude
my cheeks are laced with cognac
my hips sealed with five satin nails
i carry dreams and romance of new fools and old
flames
between the musk of fat
and the side pocket of my mink tongue

Listen to champagne bubble from this solo

Essence of Rose Solitude
veteran from texas   tiger from chicago   that's me
i cover the shrine of Duke
who like Satchmo   like Nat (King) Cole
will never die because love they say
never dies

I tell you from stair steps of these navy blue nights
these metallic snakes
these flashing fish skins
and the melodious cry of Shango
surrounded by sorrow
by the purple velvet tears
by cockhounds limping from crosses
from turtle skinned shoes
from diamond shaped skulls and canes
made from dead gazelles
wearing a face of wilting potato plants
of grey and black scissors

of bee bee shots and fifty red boils
yes the whole world loved him

I tell you from suspenders of two-timing dog odors
from inca frosted lips
nonchalant legs
i tell you from howling chant of sister Erzulie
and the exaggerated hearts of a hundred pretty
women
they loved him
this world sliding from a single flower
into a caravan of heads made into ten thousand
flowers

Ask me
Essence of Rose Solitude
chickadee from arkansas that's me
i sleep on cotton bones
cotton tails
and mellow myself in empty ballrooms
i'm no fly by night
look at my resume
I walk through the eyes of staring lizards
i throw my neck back to floorshow on bumping goat
skins
in front of my stage fright
i cover the hands of Duke who like Satchmo
like Nat (King) Cole will never die
because love they say
never dies

Tapping

for Baby Laurence, and other tap dancers

JAYNE CORTEZ

When i pat this floor
  with my tap

when i slide on air
  and fill this horn intimate with
the rhythm of my two drums

  when i cross   kick
scissor   locomotive

  take four for nothing
four we're gone

when the solidarity of my yoruba turns
join these vibrato feet
  in a Johnny Hodges lick
a chorus of insistent Charlie Parker riffs

  when i stretch out for a chromatic split
together with my double X
  converging in a quartet of circles

when I dance my spine in a slouch
  slur my lyrics with a heel slide
arch these insteps in free time

  when i drop my knees
when i fold my hands
  when i decorate this atmosphere
with a Lester Young leap and

enclose my hip like snake repetitions
in a chanting proverb
   of the freeze

I'm gonna spotlite my boogie
   in a Coltrane yelp

echo my push in a Coleman Hawkins whine

i'm gonna frog my hunch in a Duke Ellington strut

quarter stroke my rattle
   like an Albert Ayler cry

i'm gonna accent my march in a Satchmo pitch

   triple my grind in a Ma Rainey blues

i'm gonna steal no steps

   i'm gonna pay my dues

i'm gonna 1 2 3

   and let the people in the Apple
go hmmmp   hmmmmp   hmmmmmp

Sonnets Ending with a Line by Miles

STEPHEN CRAMER

i.

'Trane, of course,
       could start with a phrase & keep

         shattering it until
            he'd been through

every shuffled
       combination,

         until, fracture upon
            fracture, he blew

the phrase from every
       different angle, the run

         collapsing back into itself,
           the quick

transit of his fingertips blurred
       in the sweep

         of those furious
            calisthenics.

The man had truth to play,
       & the truth's

culmination
       is hard, so he tended

to carry on...
       When he asked his colleague

       Miles ('Trane was still a sideman)
         how to end

a solo, Miles only laughed,
       took a swig,

       & rasped, *you take the damn horn
         out your mouth.*

ii.

Hackensack,
       October '56:

       van Gelder, in the control booth,
         looked down,

asked the name of the tune—
       a fair question—

       but because Miles knew
         that if you're too quick

to name it, you can smother
       the mystery,

       he stopped, & before
         snapping off the countdown

to Jo Jones who twice hit
    the high-hat

    like a train
        pulling out of the station,

unreeled a simple skein
    of ten words that

    meant *hey, sit tight*
        & observe history.

The title? Not even *he*
    dared say it—

    we're talking *Miles,*
        the song's creator.

Just before
    he put horn to lips: *I'll play it,*

    said Miles,
        & tell you what it is later.

Coltrane's Teeth

STEPHEN CRAMER

If sweets decayed his teeth—
sugared cornbread, the candied

yam, all manner of dime
store plunder: butterscotch
disks, honey drops & peppermint,

lemon balls & root beer
barrels—if sweets decayed

his teeth until only rot clenched
to the mouthpiece,
his sound is *anything*

but sugar: in that cut
with Monk when he bursts in late

like the only party guest
you ever *really* wanted
to come, his sound is whiskey

stirred with a dull blade, rust
mixing with smoky amber,

a side of crushed chili
pepper, & vinegar rubbed into
a wound. Easy enough

to kick heroin, tobacco
& liquor, but he'd never

be able to quit the sweet
potato pie topped with whipped
cream. If sweets decayed

his teeth, then his ever widening
spiral of shattered notes (knock out

all my teeth by 30, take my
liver on your best silver
platter, yes Death, lick your fat

knuckles & give me
the prettiest shiner I ever

prayed for) his spiraling
fragments of notes turn it all into
something so sweet

I'd beg for it again & again.

Bone Music

In the 1950s, Russian hipsters found it difficult to get their hands on copies of banned Western music. So they got creative, copying bootleg records onto discarded x-rays.

STEPHEN CRAMER

i.

Inky aquariums, ghost windows:
with vinyl scarce,

we couldn't even bootleg
songs until some back-alley genius

first scavenged dumpsters
behind hospitals for this unlikely

savior. The eddy & churn
of snow, gravel underboot,

& then, among syringes
& bandages, beneath battalions

of rubber gloves & masks,
the stashed blessing of discarded x-rays.

ii.

Ah, to bring them home,
         these slides where bodies
are reduced to sooty

maps, cobalt fog inscribed
        with knots of calcium, collagen
streaks. We scissored

each sheet into a circle
        & used the blooming end
of a cigarette to burn

a center hole. Then we pressed
        the contraband of Ellington,
Armstrong, & Basie onto each

until a trumpet's ragged helix
        shimmied on a broken
femur, the cloud

of a skull with its zipper
        of teeth, the stacked
totem of a spine.

iii.

When the state caught
wind, slides grew scarce

as Siberian mangos,
& we scrounged for our own

cat scans, ultrasounds.
Aunt Sofia's MRI

is a Coleman Hawkins,
notes escaping like smoke

from the cage of her ribs.
Bring on winter, bring on

disease, & rot & fracture,
because the more broken

we become, the more music
we can spin out of our bones.

Almost Blue

Chet Baker, 1929-1988

MARK DOTY

If Hart Crane played trumpet
he'd sound like you, your horn's dark city

miraculous and broken over and over,
scale-shimmered, every harbor-flung hour

and salt-span of cabled longing,
every waterfront, the night-lovers' rendezvous.

This is the entrance
to the city of you, sleep's hellgate,

and two weeks before the casual relinquishment
of your hold—light needling

on the canal's gleaming haze
and the buds blaring like horns—

two weeks before the end, Chet,
and you're playing like anything,

singing *stay little valentine*
stay

and taking so long there are worlds sinking
between the notes, this exhalation

no longer a voice but a rush of air,
brutal, from the tunnels under the river,

the barges' late whistles you only hear
when the traffic's stilled

by snow, a city hushed and
distilled into one rush of breath,

yours, into the microphone
and the ear of that girl

in the leopard-print scarf,
one long kiss begun on the highway

and carried on dangerously,
the Thunderbird veering

on the coast road: glamor
of a perfectly splayed fender,

dazzling lipstick, a little pearl of junk,
some stretch of road breathless

and traveled into . . . Whoever she is
she's the other coast of you,

and just beyond the bridge the city's
long amalgam of ardor and indifference

is lit like a votive
then blown out. Too many rooms unrented

in this residential hotel,
and you don't want to know

why they're making that noise in the hall;
you're going to wake up in any one of the

how many ten thousand
locations of trouble and longing

going out of business forever everything must go
wake up and start wanting.

It's so much better when you don't want:
nothing falls then, nothing lost

but sleep and who wanted that
in the pearl this suspended world is,

in the warm suspension and glaze
of this song everything stays up

almost forever in the long
glide sung into the vein,

one note held almost impossibly
almost blue and the lyric takes so long

to open, a little blood
blooming: *there's no love song   finer*

but how strange the change
from major to minor

every time
we say goodbye

and you leaning into that warm
haze from the window, Amsterdam,

late afternoon glimmer
a blur of buds

breathing in the lindens
and you let go and why not

Canary

for Michael S. Harper

RITA DOVE

Billie Holiday's burned voice
had as many shadows as lights,
a mournful candelabra against a sleek piano,
the gardenia her signature under that ruined face.

(Now you're cooking, drummer to bass,
magic spoon, magic needle.
Take all day if you have to
with your mirror and your bracelet of song.)

Fact is, the invention of women under siege
has been to sharpen love in the service of myth.

If you can't be free, be a mystery.

"Coltrane, Coltrane"

SASCHA FEINSTEIN

His white-horse sleep can't be seen
on record, though Monk's double
call, loud at first, then softer,
propels him to his feet, galloping into

"Well, You Needn't." Water and God
will clean Trane's body by the end
of the year, '57, but now only
Monk's voice cuts throughout

the drug's pull: his mouthpiece
locks against rotting teeth,
sound responding in a flurry
on the beat. It's a strong solo

but not his best, not quite up to
what would come. Ten years
before his death, he's thirty-one,
just four years older than

I am now. The tape clicks into
auto-reverse, and as I drive past
Indiana's busted red barns
the album cover comes to mind:

Monk's checkered cap, dark green shades
with bamboo at the side, natty black suit,
kerchief in the pocket. On his lap,
sheet music atop an attaché case,

and he's crouched into a child's
red wagon, halfheartedly holding
the handle. He was thirty-nine.
His tilted head and time as seen by

an almost-dead cigarette lets us guess
he's had enough takes for one day.
When my friend John turned the same age—
two years before his body stopped holding

the daily quart, bloating like someone
drowned, before he dried out for good—
I gave him that record. All evening
Monk and Trane played backup

to trays of heavy crystal clinking
Jack Daniel's on ice. A nickle-dime
poker game in the corner with less
at stake, it seemed, than John's

articulately slurred argument, fate
vs free will. His art students,
some said in the morning, did well
before they switched to ouzo.

I'd left by that round. Lily,
my date, wanted some air, to walk
by the Ipswich River, then the graveyard
because, she said, there's no better relief

for the August nights. She took me
to the moonlit Mayflower stones,
our fingers inside the mossy-etched slate
to feel a time that had passed.

We crossed a path of pine needles,
tall cedar trees, some fallen

by the winter's blight, thick
and tangled wood filling the air

with carmine scent. It was there
she told me what happened to her
as a child, how her mother must have heard
father closing one door, then the other.

What could I tell her?
When I touched her hand, she kissed me
on the mouth, said she was sorry,
it was the drink, that she'd ruined

the evening and please not to think
less of her. Most had fallen asleep
when we returned. We left some people
in rocking chairs, a cardplayer

on the couch, the carpet patterned
with arms and legs like a Caravaggio,
varnish darkening as we turned off
Noguchi lamps, the overheated stereo.

Driving alone to Thelonious's septet,
I often wonder if she ever made it
South, summer in New Orleans, her paisley
blouse catching smoke, blues bands

outside the French Quarter:
shadows of trombone slides and clarinets
muting their solos across her eyes.
Before she drove away, I held her

close enough to feel against my face
her hair, curling and smelling
sweet, almost like the vapors
of whiskey, almost like cedar.

Sonnets for Stan Gage (1945-1992)

SASCHA FEINSTEIN

Your hands cracked and calloused in summer, bled
      Every winter. *That's the way it's always been,*
            You said, clutching your fingers in a mottled
White towel. All of your unspoken
      Words—the angular elbows and snapped wrists—
            Resonate in memory like cymbals left
Unstruck, forever anticipating the stick's
      Crash. Damn it, Stan. You thought death
            Was some young drummer you could cut, the way
You kept outplaying fate with heroin
      Overdoses, a mugger's four-inch blade
            In your chest which now I can only see in
My mind heaving. The clean linoleum tile.
      A nurse washing her hands. The cold bed rail.

Floodlight shadow. Your shoes are stroking
      The platform's edge. Two hours before the gig—
            The drums HAVE to be intimidating!—
And because you think they're not you take a swig
      Of J.D. from a shiny flask. But they were.
            This was pain: each platinum strike drove nails
Into my head. ("STAN!") I'm still caught there,
      Pressed against the auditorium wall,
            Twitching as warm-up shots detonated
My chest. ("STAN! You've made the clock jump
      Forward!") *Yeah, but did they INTIMIDATE?*
            Sticks on the drum-kit rug, you walk to the front
Of the stage, fingers slicing the air,
      Flicking blood across a row of wooden chairs.

With young people the heart keeps beating even
      After other organs decay, your mother told me
            In the hours when tubes of pure oxygen
Failed to purify your liver, your kidneys—
      Just days after being admitted, amused,
            Almost, that you'd finally quit smoking. (And what
Hipster wrote, "Drummers and poets are used
      Like ashtrays YES"?) I loved how with cigarettes
            You'd sketch Emily Remler's guitar solos
At Fat Tuesday's, and you wanted every note
      She played. *Can you believe it? Thirty-two!*
            ("Was it a heart attack? Someone wrote—")
No, speedball. Impish smile. *But okay, sure—*
      I mean, you know—EVERYONE dies of heart failure.

I expect to see at dusk your rhythmic
      Figure strutting Main Street, on the way
            To some "no cake" gig, shades and hair slicked
Clean as your black suit, your grin—*Hey, babe!*—
      And news of a book on the twenties
            Art scene in Paris. You'll tell me you're sure
I won't believe it. And you'll tell me jazz
      Is just another language for the curve
            In a woman's dress photographed from behind.
And look at this. And look at this. And look
      At this. But right now I can't even define
            What loss feels like. Sycamore leaves. My rake
Scrapes up fallen sticks. I feel my dry skin
      Chafe from the air. My hands are bleeding.

Blues Villanelle for Sonny Criss

SASCHA FEINSTEIN

A lunar eclipse, and your solos spread
across wild clover as I exhale
and try not to think of the gun at your head,
how we say but rarely believe, "You can't be dead

if you're on record." Your alto wails
to the moon's elision, the solo spread
against the splintering woodshed.
It's '57, one year before jail,

twenty before the gun's at your head
and you're my age playing "Calidad,"
"Willow Weep for Me," "Love for Sale,"
as the brief clips from your solo spread

the graying moon like cigarettes
in walnut-paneled dives, overpriced cocktails
cold as the gun you'll hold to your head.
But I'm trying not to see that, trying instead

to let the bass and chromatic scales
eclipse you, solo, outspread.
I'm trying not to think. The gun's at your head.

Christmas Eve

Sascha Feinstein

You'd think they'd be with family,
At a party, out of town, but it's Miles,
Monk, Bags, Percy, and Klook
In Van Gelder's New Jersey studio.
Twenty-five years later, I fall for
A woman who has both out-of-print LPs,
Together a collage of tunes
From that gig, two cuts of "The Man I Love"
With a mumbled argument that stops
The first take. We tried so many times
To make out the words, unable to hear
Enough through her speakers, pressing together.
Young love. 1954: my parents
Hadn't met, couldn't imagine
The failure of their first marriages
Or why my mother would turn to painting,
To my father's classes, their attraction
Unspoken. Love came to them the way
Miles punctured the air with notes soft enough
To hold a woman, lines floating somewhere
Between Jackson's vibraharp mellifluous
Against Monk's dissonant chords. Late
December. I won't be born for nine years.
It's the holiday, though Dad doesn't know it
Yet, that deadens what's left of the marriage,
Days he won't talk about unless
Memory triggers a joke: what not to say
To a wife, how not to listen when you should.
This is the holiday my mother decides
She won't return to the U.S. until
Divorce papers arrive signed, but comes back
For reasons she doesn't understand,
Facing it. Streetlamps on her lost complexion.

And who decided to tint the black-and-white
Cover photo of Miles with eyes closed, horn
And harmon mute now sickly fluorescent?
No snow in Hackensack, but it's cold and
Monk's pissed 'cause Miles asks him to lay out
During trumpet solos. They have words.
Some in the studio leave for dinner
And don't return, regretting forever
Not hearing live the improvisations
That swelled from angry respect and need.
Across the Hudson, my father attends,
By himself, a party in the Village.
My mom's there also, though she's with the husband
She doesn't want, hangs her head
Until hair hides her face, and my father
Doesn't even see her. I wonder, sometimes,
What he would have said, what she would have heard,
If she could have answered at all and could he
Withstand pockets of silence the way Miles
Did not: the second take of "The Man I Love"
Where impatience and Thelonious's time
Cause the trumpet to enter mid-chorus.
Monk hammers the bridge, consumes the space,
Cuts him. It's more volatile than their fight
On the first take where Bags pedaltones
The intro, his phrases fracturing
To Monk's mutiny, momentary chaos:
"When you want me to come in, man?" and
"Man, the cat's cuttin' the thing," and
"I don't know when to come in, man," and
"I stopped, too, everybody—," then Miles,
"*Shhhhhhhhhhh*," hushes the group, and because
He knows for some reason this is important,
That it's part of what makes the music, turns
To the booth, to Van Gelder nervously
Recording the gig, and says, "Hey, Rudy,
Put this on the record—*all of it.*"

Everything Happens to Me, 1965

SASCHA FEINSTEIN

i. Cannonball Adderley at the Capitol Recording
   Studio, New York City

   I can appreciate what you're saying,
and I know Bird got a lot of heat

for his string sessions. I've come to accept
   ignorance—no offense. My playing's

   not intended to please, necessarily.
As I said in the notes for the album:

This is simply one assault upon
   the tyranny of style, 'cause tyranny

fuels this LP. *Domination.*
   Consider that title, you dig? Reread
     what I've written. There's nothing technical

'bout my comments on these compositions:
   The tyrant will probably turn out to be
     music itself—that which dominates us all.

ii. Marion Brown at *The Star Ledger* Offices, Newark

   My best year, yeah. I've been in the studio
a lot. But I don't sing. (Listen, my brother—

if you're gonna cut the white reporters,
   do your homework. What'd your boss tell you?

   That I was a woman?) [Laughs.] I just made
a quartet album—my first as leader.

Recorded with Trane earlier this year—.
   What's that? C-O-L-T-R-A-N-E . . .

Archie Shepp's *Fire Music*: that was very
   intense. We played "Malcolm, Semper Malcolm"
      as "Funeral"—for Evers. Medgar Evers.

It was the middle of February.
   We sure felt it . . . Then they wasted Brother Malcolm,
      though that was five long days later.

iii. Ornette Coleman on the Ferry from Denmark to Sweden

   Let me get this right. Forward to the border.
Stop. Cars detach. Half the train backs out. Tracks lock,

and then the front cars—with us—cross the dock
   into the ferry. That right? And we order

   food on the boat? Very cool . . . Now, tomorrow—
what's the place called? Golden Circle?—we play

nothing from last night's gig in Tivoli:
   "Lonely Woman." "Falling Star"—out. Only new

compositions. A kind of call and response
   to *all* of this: "European Echoes."
      "Faces and Places." "Snowflakes and Sunshine."

Train brakes on train tracks spiked to the deck. *Sounds.*
    We'll play travel *and* the moment, you know?
        "The Riddle": How does a boat swallow a train?

iv. Sonny Criss at Shelly's Manne Hole, Hollywood

    Next day, I got all these telephone calls—
You okay? You see all that shit last night?

Watts . . . Never would have imagined it.
    It's like I explained to Hampton Hawes:

    I saw the flames, grabbed a fifth of J&B,
a folding chair, took 'em out to the lawn,

got comfortable. Felt like Nero! By dawn
    the sky was all speckled in a blackish green

like, I don't know—like Bessie's blues,
    or the cargo hold of some terrible slave
        ship. But it was funny, too. What a sight . . .

I just recorded with Hawes back in June:
    "When Sunny Gets Blue." "The Masquerade
        Is Over." Boy, did we get *that* right.

v. Paul Desmond in Benjamin's Tavern, Stratford, Ontario

    So you can argue a dry martini
can't *sound* like a horn, that it has more edge

than my sound. Actually, I've come to regret
    the line itself—but not dry martinis!

    Just last week, in Brussels, Dave called for "Blue
Rondo a la Turk," and Morello limped

toward the stand, but I just couldn't
    leave that bar: Belgian blonde, late afternoon...

That first sip makes any gal your greatest date.
    Imperfections vanish like "My Funny
        Valentine"—the changes from the bridge on out.

Of course, by your fifth it's too late:
    your funny valentine has not only
        changed a hair for you, she's totally wigged out.

vi. Eric Dolphy (1928-1964) in Charles Mingus's
        Dream, Manhattan

    It's all sugar here: sugar clouds, sugar
women. You can taste your mouthpiece, Charles.

Sit at that black Formica table while
    I pour sugar from my palm. Can you hear

    the dancing grains? Think of a winter
ice storm, except it's the end of June

and you're lost in the streets of Berlin.
    When the sugar loses sound, you enter,

very softly, as though fingering patterns
in this sweet sand. And now, the melody:
D minor seventh, then a sudden leap—

Mingus, humming Dolphy's dreamsong, turns
on his back, yells, *Eric, Wait!—I'm not ready,*
then, *Sue. Wake up. You gotta get me back to sleep.*

vii. Lee Konitz at Johanneshov Isstadium, Stockholm

Of course it's great to play with Bill Evans,
and, yeah, I'm sure he's still grieving. I mean,

when someone's so gifted and young—Scottie
just made twenty-five—and he's your left hand,

and then he's gone in a crash, you question
if you'll ever sound right again, if you'll

be a soul without a soul mate. Life's cruel . . .
But what about *this* bass player. Exceptional

timing. Trust me if you can't hear it: this Dane's
beautiful. Understand? You've got to feel
the present and think of the future. This kid's

nineteen, for Christ's sake. Write down his name:
Niels-Henning Ørsted Pedersen . . . Hey Bill,
what do you call an O with a slash through it?

viii. Charlie Mariano at the Berklee School of Music, Boston

   That was February—two days after
the assassination of Malcolm X.

I was the only white guy there. My sax
   felt three times as heavy. Maybe four.

   But Elvin and Hank, Richard and Roland—
they said nothing. It was all about our

music . . . Toshiko and our daughter—
   we named her Monday—they're still in Japan.

She's about to record some of my tunes.
   Big band. The horn section's all Japanese:
      Shigeo Suzuki. "Sleepy" Matsumoto.

They shouldn't have much trouble laying down
   the charts. Can't speak for the rest. I mean,
      there's a chasm between technique and soul.

ix. Jackie McLean in Rudy Van Gelder's Studio, Englewood
   Cliffs

   No, no, no, no, *no*. Four bars, ten beats—
everybody in unison—horns, drums,

everybody—and *then* the pickup.
   Here, bracket those bars—two sets of quintuplets.

What? Look, it's not one ... It's not one ... Jack!
Tell Larry and Larry to shut up. *Man* ...

It's not one person's *fault*. You all got that?
   Okay? We'll just do another damn take.

(The Man's gonna take everything anyway,
   right? You're fighting like you're fighting for *justice*
     instead of focusing on the matter

at hand: *this composition*. Right?) Okay.
   Quiet ... "Jacknife." Take *eleven* ... Jesus,
     Charles. Why'd you write such a motherfucker?

x. Art Pepper in the Exercise Yard of San Quentin State Prison

Stupid goddam parole violation.
That's all—or at least the most of it.

I was at a local club, my first gig
   after getting out. Felt real edgy. Then

   a waitress leans down and says, "There's fuzz
in this place," and then I see them staring

into my horn ... "Everything Happens to Me"—
   You know the tune? [Sings:] *Your answer was*

"Good-bye," and there was even postage due ...
   We played that beautifully. Long set, no breaks—
     I think we played for almost two hours

without a single break—but I knew
   they'd wait me out, so finally I said, "Thanks,"
     and stepped off the stand, into the applause.

Meet Me at the Lighthouse

Dana Gioia

Meet me at the Lighthouse in Hermosa Beach,
That shabby nightclub on its foggy pier.
Let's aim for the summer of '71,
When all our friends were young and immortal.

I'll pick up the cover charge, find us a table,
And order a round of their watery drinks.
Let's savor the smoke of that sinister century,
Perfume of tobacco in the tangy salt air.

The crowd will be quiet—only ghosts at the bar—
So you, old friend, won't feel out of place.
You need a night out from that dim subdivision.
Tell Mr. Bones you'll be back before dawn.

The club has booked the best talent in Tartarus.
Gerry, Cannonball, Hampton, and Stan,
With Chet and Art, those gorgeous greenhorns—
The swinging-masters of our West Coast soul.

Let the All-Stars shine from that jerrybuilt stage.
Let their high notes shimmer above the cold waves.
Time and the tide are counting the beats.
Death the collector is keeping the tab.

Dear John, Dear Coltrane

Michael S. Harper

a love supreme, a love supreme
a love supreme, a love supreme

Sex fingers toes
in the marketplace
near your father's church
in Hamlet, North Carolina—
witness to this love
in this calm fallow
of these minds,
there is no substitute for pain:
genitals gone or going,
seed burned out,
you tuck the roots in the earth,
turn back, and move
by the river through the swamps,
singing *a love supreme, a love supreme;*
what does it all mean?
Loss, so great each black
woman expects your failure
in mute change, the seed gone.
You plod up into the electric city—
your song now crystal and
the blues. You pick up the horn
with some will and blow
into the freezing night:
a love supreme, a love supreme—

Dawn comes and you cook
up the thick sin 'tween
impotence and death, fuel
the tenor sax cannibal
heart, genital and sweat

that makes you clean—
a love supreme, a love supreme—

Why you so black?
cause I am
why you so funky?
cause I am
why you so black?
cause I am
why you so sweet?
cause I am
why you so black?
cause I am
a love supreme, a love supreme:

So sick
you couldn't play *Naima,*
so flat we ached
for song you'd concealed
with your own blood,
your diseased liver gave
out its purity,
the inflated heart
pumps out, the tenor kiss,
tenor love:
a love supreme, a love supreme—
a love supreme, a love supreme—

Jazzonia

LANGSTON HUGHES

Oh, silver tree!
Oh, shining rivers of the soul!

In a Harlem cabaret
Six long-headed jazzers play.
A dancing girl whose eyes are bold
Lifts high a dress of silken gold.

Oh, singing tree!
Oh, shining rivers of the soul!

Were Eve's eyes
In the first garden
Just a bit too bold?
Was Cleopatra gorgeous
In a gown of gold?

Oh, shining tree!
Oh, silver rivers of the soul!

In a whirling cabaret
Six long-headed jazzers play.

Trumpet Player

LANGSTON HUGHES

The Negro
With the trumpet at his lips
Has dark moons of weariness
Beneath his eyes
Where the smoldering memory
Of slave ships
Blazed to the crack of whips
About his thighs.

The Negro
With the trumpet at his lips
Has a head of vibrant hair
Tamed down,
Patent-leathered now
Until it gleams
Like jet—
Were jet a crown.

The music
From the trumpet at his lips
Is honey
Mixed with liquid fire.
The rhythm
From the trumpet at his lips
Is ecstasy
Distilled from old desire—

Desire
That is longing for the moon
Where the moonlight's but a spotlight
In his eyes,
Desire

That is longing for the sea
Where the sea's a bar-glass
Sucker size.

The Negro
With the trumpet at his lips
Whose jacket
Has a *fine* one-button roll,
Does not know
Upon what riff the music slips
Its hypodermic needle
To his soul—

But softly
As the tune comes from his throat
Trouble
Mellows to a golden note.

Song for Billie Holiday

Langston Hughes

What can purge my heart
    Of the song
    And the sadness?
What can purge my heart
    But the song
    Of the sadness?
What can purge my heart
    Of the sadness
    Of the song?

Do not speak of sorrow
With dust in her hair,
Or bits of dust in eyes
A chance wind blows there.
The sorrow that I speak of
Is dusted with despair.

Voice of muted trumpet,
Cold brass in warm air.
Bitter television blurred
By sound that shimmers—
    Where?

Lost Fugue for Chet

Chet Baker, Amsterdam, 1988

LYNDA HULL

A single spot slides the trumpet's flare then stops
    at that face, the extraordinary ruins thumb-marked
with the hollows of heroin, the rest chiaroscuroed.
    Amsterdam, the final gig, canals & countless

stone bridges arc, glimmered in lamps. Later this week
    his Badlands face, handsome in a print from thirty
years ago, will follow me from the obituary page
    insistent as windblown papers by the black cathedral

of St. Nicholas standing closed today: pigeon shit
    & feathers, posters swathing tarnished doors, a litter
of syringes. Junkies cloud the gutted railway station blocks
    & dealers from doorways call *coca, heroina,* some throaty

foaming harmony. A measured inhalation, again
    the sweet embouchure, metallic, wet stem. Ghostly,
the horn's improvisations purl & murmur
    the narrow *strasses* of *Rosse Buurt*, the district rife

with purse-snatchers, women alluring, desolate, poised
    in blue windows, Michelangelo boys, hair spilling
fluent running chords, mares' tails in the sky green
    & violet. So easy to get lost, these cavernous

brown cafés. Amsterdam, & its spectral fogs, its
    bars & softly shifting tugboats. He builds once more
the dense harmonic structure, the gabled houses.
    Let's get lost. Why court the brink & then step back?

After surviving, what arrives? So what's the point
    when there are so many women, creamy callas with single
furled petals turning in & upon themselves
    like variation, nights when the horn's coming

genius riffs, metal & spit, that rich consuming rush
    of good dope, a brief languor burnishing
the groin, better than any sex. Fuck Death.
    In the audience, there's always this gaunt man, cigarette

in hand, black Maserati at the curb, waiting,
    the fast ride through mountain passes, descending with
no rails between asphalt & precipice. Inside, magnetic
    whispering *take me there, take me.* April, the lindens

& horse chestnuts flowering, cold white blossoms
    on the canal. He's lost as he hears those inner voicings,
a slurred veneer of chords, molten, fingering
    articulate. His glance below Dutch headlines, the fall

"accidental" from a hotel sill. Too loaded. What do you do
    at the brink? Stepping back in time, I can only
imagine the last hit, lilies insinuating themselves
    up your arms, leaves around your face, one hand vanishing

sabled to shadow. The newsprint photo & I'm trying
    to recall names, songs, the sinuous figures, but facts
don't matter, what counts is out of pained dissonance,
    the sick vivid green of backstage bathrooms, out of

broken rhythms—and I've never forgotten, never—
    *this is the tied-off vein, this is 3 A.M. terror
thrumming, this is the carnation of blood clouding
    the syringe,* you shaped *summer rains across the quays*

of Paris, flame suffusing jade against a girl's
     dark ear. From the trumpet, pawned, redeemed, pawned again
you formed one wrenching blue arrangement, a phrase endlessly
     complicated as that twilit dive through smoke, applause,

the pale hunted rooms. Cold chestnuts flowering April
     & you're falling from heaven in a shower of eighth notes
to the cobbled street below & foaming dappled horses
     plunge beneath the still green waters of the Grand Canal.

Ornithology

Lynda Hull

Gone to seed, ailanthus, the poverty
  tree. Take a phrase, then
fracture it, the pods' gaudy nectarine shades
    ripening to parrots taking flight, all crest
and tail feathers.
                 A musical idea.
                                Macaws
   scarlet and violet,
                     tangerine as a song
the hue of sunset where my street becomes water

and down shore this phantom city skyline's
  mere hazy silhouette. The alto's
liquid geometry weaves *a way of thinking,*
   a way of breaking
synchronistic
              through time
                       so the girl
   on the corner
              has the bones of my face,
the old photos, beneath the Kansas City hat,

black fedora lifting hair off my neck
  cooling the sweat of a night-long tidal
pull from bar to bar the night we went
   to find Bird's grave. Eric's chartreuse
perfume. That
           poured-on dress
                  I lived days

and nights inside,
                    made love
and slept in, a mesh and slur of zipper

down the back. Women smoked the boulevards
    with gardenias after-hours, asphalt shower-
slick, ozone charging air with sixteenth
        notes, that endless convertible ride to find
the grave
            whose sleep and melody
                                wept neglect
enough to torch us
                    for a while
through snare-sweep of broom on pavement,

the rumpled musk of lover's sheets, charred
    cornices topping crosstown gutted buildings.
Torches us still—cat screech, matte blue steel
    of pistol stroked across the victim's cheek
where fleet shoes
                jazz this dark
                                and peeling
    block, that one.
                    Vine Street, Olive.
We had the music, but not the pyrotechnics—

rhinestone straps lashing my shoes, heels sinking
    through earth and Eric in casual drag,
mocha cheekbones rouged, that flawless
    plummy mouth. A style for moving,
heel tap and
            lighter flick,
                        lion moan
    of buses pulling away
                            through the static
brilliant fizz of taffeta on nyloned thighs.

Light mist, etherous, rinsed our faces
    and what happens when
you touch a finger to the cold stone
    that jazz and death played
down to?
            Phrases.
                    Take it all
    and break forever—
                    a man
with gleaming sax, an open sill in summertime,

and the fire-escape's iron zigzag tumbles
    crazy notes to a girl cooling her knees,
wearing one of those dresses no one wears
    anymore, darts and spaghetti straps, glitzy
fabrics foaming
                an iron bedstead.
                            The horn's
    alarm, then fluid brass chromatics.
                            Extravagant
ailanthus, the courtyard's poverty tree is spike
and wing, slate-blue
                mourning dove,
                        sudden cardinal
flame.

If you don't live it, it won't come out your horn.

Hollywood Jazz

LYNDA HULL

Who says it's cool says wrong.
  For it rises from the city's
    sweltering geometry of rooms,

fire escapes, and flares from the heels
  of corner boys on Occidental
    posing with small-time criminal

intent—all pneumatic grace. This
  is the music that plays at the moment
    in every late-night *noir* flick

when the woman finds herself alone, perfectly
  alone in a hotel room before a man
    whose face is so shadowed as to be

invisible, one more bedroom arsonist
  seeing nothing remotely
    cool: a woman in a cage

of half-light, Venetian blinds.
  This is where jazz blooms, in the hook
    and snag of her zipper opening to

an enfilade of trumpets. Her dress
  falls in a dizzy indigo riff.
    I know her vices are minor: sex,

forgetfulness, the desire to be someone,
  anyone else. On the landing, the man
    pauses before descending
one more flight. Checks his belt. Adjusts

the snap brim over his face. She smoothes
   her platinum hair and smokes a Lucky

to kill his cologne. And standing there
   by the window in her slip, midnight blue,
      the stockings she did not take off,

she is candescent, her desolation
   a music so voluptuous I want
      to linger with her. And if I do not

turn away from modesty or shame,
   I'm in this for keeps, flying with her
      into fear's random pivot where each article

glistens like evidence: the tube of lipstick,
   her discarded earrings. When she closes
      her eyes, she hears the streetcar's

nocturne up Jackson, a humpbacked sedan
   rounding the corner from now
      to that lavish void of tomorrow,

a sequence of rooms: steam heat, modern,
   2 bucks. Now listen. Marimbas.
      His cologne persists, a redolence

of fire alarms, and Darling,
   there are no innocents here, only
      dupes, voyeurs. On the stairs

he flicks dust from his alligator
   shoes. I stoop to straighten
      the seams of my stockings, and

when I meet him in the shadows
   of the stairwell, clarinets whisper
      Here, take my arm. Walk with me.

Billie in Silk

ANGELA JACKSON

I have nothing to say to you, Billie Holiday.
You do not look at me when I try to speak to you.
You cannot look me in the eye. Your eyes
look elsewhere.
Your steamy mouth sewn up with red tears
is poised to speak
to someone.
The orchid in your hair grows, grows like
a spider turning herself inside out.
The shadow hangs
into your eye.

I have smiled the way you
do not smile.
I was just out of love,
and cold.
I was naked, beyond caring.
My smile, like yours, was a wry line
beside my steamy mouth.
My eyes, like yours, didn't look at me,
I only saw the fall
from
grace.

(You lay down with music in the leaves.
You wrapped him in leaves, in sheets.
Your legs lindyed around him. Young
then old. Do not be deceived. The
thunder of the spider is no small
thing. You had your way with music,
and ate him. The memory hot
in your belly. Ours.)

You never want to let her leave.
She. The voice deceives.
You could hurt it.
It would kill you
too.
The dragline seeking
curving above Surprise.
Below
Just so.
Size is not the issue.
Volume not
the question. A hairline
fracture in the Silence
in which nothing rests.
The voice deceives.
Every thing
swings.

I have something to say to you, Billie Holiday.
Sew up your breathing, then send it back to me.
Fluent and ruminating the source of such anguish.

Look into my eyes.

If only it were not so lonely to be black and bruised
by an early-morning dream
that lifts the mouth to sing.

Here is an orchid, spideresque-petaled, glorious,
full of grace.

My mouth is on fire. Let it burn.

Black Orchid

Miles Davis, New York, August, 1950

DAVID JAUSS

Tonight he's playing the Black Orchid,
the old Onyx where before his habit
he played with Bird, looking cleaner
than a motherfucker, Brooks Brothers suit,
marcelled hair, trumpet floating over
that hurricane of sixteenth notes no one
could have played sober—19, a dentist's son,
on stage with *Bird* and laying down shit
nobody ever heard before or since!—but now
his fourth cap of heroin's wearing off,
its petals closing up inside his chest so tight
he can barely breathe. Drunk again,
Bud hangs heavy over the keys, left hand
jabbing chords that break his right hand's
waterfall arpeggios: "April in Paris,"
and that strangely tropical odor of coconut
and lime in rum comes back to Miles,
the smell of Paris, Juliette Greco's sweet lips
as she sang, each syllable a kiss
for him alone. *Juliette,*
his trumpet moans, *her small hands*
on the small of my back, long hair black
on the white pillow . . . Even Sartre
tried to talk him into marrying her
but he'd gone back to America, to Irene,
and a habit. And though numerology proved
he was a perfect six, the Devil's number,
he drove the Blue Demon, top down, to East St. Louis,
Irene silent beside him, the kids crying
in the back seat, one thousand miles

to escape heroin and the memory
of Juliette's white shoulder. But now
he's back, alone, long sleeves
hiding fresh tracks on his forearms,
and it's not Bird but Sonny who's unraveling
the melody, looking in it for a way
to put it all back together again.
Then Wardell leaps in, *This is it, man,*
can't you hear it? They're dueling
like Ground Hog and Baby, the junky tapdancers
who buck-and-winged for dope on the sidewalk
outside Minton's, feet turning desperation
into music, and Miles joins them, his mute
disguising the notes he fluffs. He sounds
as bad as Fats, last May when they recorded
Birdland All-Stars. Glassy-eyed, nose running,
Fat Girl had to strain to hit notes
he used to own. 26 and just two
months to live. *I'm going to kick this shit,*
Miles vowed the night Fats died,
but here he is, blowing a borrowed horn
because he pawned his own to play
a syringe's one-valve song. If only
he'd stayed, if only he'd never come back . . .
Behind him, Art plays Paris dark
as a jungle, and Miles falls into her pale arms,
the dark hotel room, and he's lost, lost
and free, released from some burden he's borne
across the ocean, to this bed, this woman,
a burden that, lifting, lifts him
like music, one clear unwavering note piercing
the silence that defines it . . .
When he tries to explain, she tells him
that's *existentialisme.* "Existential,
shit," he says, "Let's fuck."
And she laughs, her mouth a red flower
opening under his. Then he kisses
two whole notes out of his horn, their beauty

painful as they vanish into the swirling
smoke of the Orchid, each note
unfurling, an orchid itself, its petals
falling and settling on the nodding heads
of grinning white Americans
who will never understand jazz, or Paris,
or him. He closes his eyes,
and for as long as his solo lasts,
it's not August, it's not New York,
and he is not dying.

J.J. Johnson Changes Tempo

A. Van Jordan

When J.J. raises his horn to hip lips,
the loss of Vivian laces each note.
He holds that slide like
it's her hand
and moonbeams burrow
through smoke-filled rooms,
a hundred legs dance on brass shimmers,
a thousand snap dragons swallow low notes.

While other cats rush
in blaring through the cursive bore J.J.,
smooth as long shaved legs,
whispers through its hollow body.

If he plays with an open bell,
every smile has a gold tooth.
If he uses a mute,
men sob into calloused hands.

But when Vivian was at his side,
when the tempo rang like an eighth note
chain gang, when jealous lovers reached for razors
and hired guns pulled up chairs,
even J.J.'s whisper,
which filled men's lungs like a deep kiss,
and wrapped women in two strong arms,
could only be explained by his slide
trombone fluttering like a satyr's tongue.

Vapors of Sidney Bechet

born May 14, 1897, New Orleans; died May 14, 1959, Paris

A. Van Jordan

If he gargles mood in his mouth
leaving options open to the reed,
        time and space lose significance.

Let's call this, the way a sound is born,
        the way a worksong becomes blues,
ragtime becomes a living,
        blows over an ocean and becomes "art."

What can we call wind that picks up
        blue notes with needle and thread,
with reeds of black or brass? What flows into
        the Embassy Club picking up the scent of imported perfume
or a dance hall lifting sawdust and obscenities?

        Call it a "remembering song."
Call it life's crossroads.
        Something more than the whim of wind,
than a love of music in dark crevices
        and foreign tongues. Let dreams travel
on a staff of sixteenth notes, let them rest
        legato, give them stomps, blues, and ballads.

Let the song change like love that's gone crazy
        baby teeth in a big boy's head,
shoes on a wealthy woman.
        If it gives birth and death on the same day in May,
haunts and hums in Creole and blues,
        if it growls and swishes in your ear
like a lover's promise,

call it something that measures distance
beyond the reach of roots.

If it's soprano wind through a saxophone,
        swirled first over Sidney's lips,
call it a man who's made up his mind
        to blow something as beautiful
as a jazzman dancing on a compass.

For Dinah Washington

ALLISON JOSEPH

Born poor, born colored, born Ruth Jones,
she had to become Dinah, had to show
that a tubby girl from the Tuscaloosa projects
could be queen, wear a tiara like nobody's
business, a slick chick on the mellow side,
making melodies behave when men didn't.
She brought gospel from the churches
to the clubs, sang blues behind her mama's
back to make cash money so they'd never
have to share a pair of stockings again,
changed her name to front jazz bands—
Hampton's, Lucky Thompson's All-Stars,
Tab Smith's. Think of her in furs, satin,
making a fool of Brook Benton on corny
duets like "Baby, You've Got What It
Takes." She complains at record's end:
You're in my spot again, mad he'd even
dare sing over her lines. Don't think of her
broken, broke, desperate from too much
drink and too many diets, too many one-
nighters, husbands—seven, eight, or nine,
depending on the bio. Don't think of her
as a maid's child, drifter's daughter, dead
from pills and booze. Think of her, gutsy
and bejeweled, salty and Southern on "Evil
Gal Blues," sultry-smooth on "What A
Diff'rence A Day Made." Think of her,
striking on stage at the Regal Theatre,
striding out there like she owned it, owned us.

Choruses 239-241 of *Mexico City Blues*

JACK KEROUAC

239th Chorus

Charley Parker Looked like Buddha.
Charley Parker, who recently died
Laughing at a juggler on the TV
after weeks of strain and sickness,
was called the Perfect Musician.
And his expression on his face
Was as calm, beautiful, and profound
As the image of the Buddha
Represented in the East, the lidded eyes,
The expression that says "All Is Well"
—This was what Charley Parker
Said when he played, All is Well.
You had the feeling of early-in-the-morning
Like a hermit's joy, or like
                        the perfect cry
Of some wild gang at a jam session,
"Wail, Wop" —Charley burst
His lungs to reach the speed
Of what the speedsters wanted
And what they wanted
Was his Eternal Slowdown.
A great musician and a great
                        creator of forms
That ultimately find expression
In mores and what have you.

240th Chorus

Musically as important as Beethoven,
Yet not regarded as such at all,
A genteel conductor of string
                              orchestras
In front of which he stood,
Proud and calm, like a leader
                              of music
In the Great Historic World Night,
And wailed his little saxophone,
The alto, with piercing clear
                              lament
In perfect tune & shining harmony,
Toot—as listeners reacted
Without showing it, and began talking
And soon the whole joint is rocking
And everybody talking and Charley
                              Parker
Whistling them on to the brink of eternity
With his Irish St Patrick
                     patootle stick,
And like the holy piss we blop
And we plop in the waters of
                              slaughter
And white meat, and die
One after one, in time.

241st Chorus

And how sweet a story it is
When you hear Charley Parker
                         tell it.
Either on records or at sessions,
Or at official bits in clubs,
Shots in the arm for the wallet,
Gleefully he Whistled the
                       perfect
                       horn.

Anyhow, made no difference.

Charley Parker, forgive me—
Forgive me for not answering your eyes—
For not having made an indication
Of that which you can devise—
Charley Parker, pray for me—
Pray for me, and everybody
In the Nirvanas of your brain
Where you hide, indulgent and huge,
No longer Charley Parker
But the secret unsayable name
That carries with it merit
Not to be measured from here
To up, down, east or west—
—Charley Parker lay the bane,
   off me and every body

For Eric Dolphy

ETHERIDGE KNIGHT

on flute
spinning   spinning   spinning
love
thru/ out
the universe

i
know
exactly
whut chew mean
man

you like
titi
my sister
who never expressed LOVE
in words (like the white folks always   d
she would sit in the corner   o
and cry   i
everytime   n
ah   g
got a whuppin

Jazz Drummer

Etheridge Knight

MAX ROACH
   has fire and steel in his hands,
   rides high, is a Makabele warrior,
   tastes death on his lips, beats babies
   from worn out wombs,
                grins with grace,
   and cries in the middle of his eyes.

MAX ROACH
   thumps the big circle in bare feet,
   opens wide the big arms,
   and like the sea
          calls us all.

Elegy for Thelonious

Yusef Komunyakaa

Damn the snow.
Its senseless beauty
pours a hard light
through the hemlock.
Thelonious is dead. Winter
drifts in the hourglass;
notes pour from the brain cup.
Damn the alley cat
wailing a muted dirge
off Lenox Ave.
Thelonious is dead.
Tonight's a lazy rhapsody of shadows
swaying to blue vertigo
& metaphysical funk.
Black trees in the wind.
Crepuscule with Nellie
plays inside the bowed head.
"Dig the Man Ray of piano!"
O Satisfaction,
hot fingers blur
on those white rib keys.
Coming on the Hudson.
Monk's Dream.
The ghost of bebop
from 52nd Street,
footprints in the snow.
Damn February.
Let's go to Minton's
& play "modern malice"
till daybreak. Lord,
there's Thelonious
wearing that old funky hat
pulled down over his eyes.

February in Sydney

Yusef Komunyakaa

Dexter Gordon's tenor sax
plays "April in Paris"
inside my head all the way back
on the bus from Double Bay.
Round Midnight, the '50s,
cool cobblestone streets
resound footsteps of Bebop
musicians with whiskey-laced voices
from a boundless dream in French.
Bud, Prez, Webster, & The Hawk,
their names run together riffs.
Painful gods jive talk through
bloodstained reeds & shiny brass
where music is an anesthetic.
Unreadable faces from the human void
float like torn pages across the bus
windows. An old anger drips into my throat,
& I try thinking something good,
letting the precious bad
settle to the salty bottom.
Another scene keeps repeating itself:
I emerge from the dark theatre,
passing a woman who grabs her red purse
& hugs it to her like a heart attack.
Tremolo. Dexter comes back to rest
behind my eyelids. A loneliness
lingers like a silver needle
under my black skin,
as I try to feel how it is
to scream for help through a horn.

Blue Light Lounge Sutra for the Performance Poets at Harold Park Hotel

Yusef Komunyakaa

the need gotta be
so deep words can't
answer simple questions
all night long notes
stumble off the tongue
& color the air indigo
so deep fragments of gut
& flesh cling to the song
you gotta get into it
so deep salt crystalizes on eyelashes
the need gotta be
so deep you can vomit up ghosts
& not feel broken
till you are no more
than a half ounce of gold
in painful brightness
you gotta get into it
blow that saxophone
so deep all the sex & dope in this world
can't erase your need
to howl against the sky
the need gotta be
so deep you can't
just wiggle your hips
& rise up out of it
chaos in the cosmos
modern man in the pepperpot
you gotta get hooked
into every hungry groove
so deep the bomb locked
in rust opens like a fist

into it into it so deep
rhythm is pre-memory
the need gotta be basic
animal need to see
& know the terror
we are made of honey
cause if you wanna dance
this boogie be ready
to let the devil use your head
for a drum

Testimony

YUSEF KOMUNYAKAA

I

He hopped boxcars to Chitown
late fall, just a few steps
ahead of the hawk. After
sleepwalking to the 65 Club,
he begged Goon for a chance
to sit in with a borrowed sax.
He'd paid his dues for years
blowing ravenous after-hours
till secrets filled with blues
rooted in Mississippi mud;
he confessed to Budd Johnson
that as a boy playing stickball,
sometimes he'd spy in a window
as they rehearsed back in K.C.

It was Goon who took him home,
gave him clothes & a clarinet.
Maybe that's when he first
played laughter & crying
at the same time. Nights
sucked the day's marrow
till the hibernating moon grew
fat with lies & chords. Weeks
later, with the horn hocked,
he was on a slow Greyhound
headed for the Big Apple,
& "Honeysuckle Rose"
blossomed into body language,
driven by a sunset on the Hudson.

II

Washing dishes at Jimmy's
Chicken Shack from midnight
to eight for nine bucks a week
just to hear Art Tatum's keys,
he simmered in jubilation
for over three months. After
a tango palace in Times Square
& jam sessions at Clark Monroe's,
in the back room of a chili house
on "Cherokee," he could finally play
everything inside his head,
the melodic line modulating
through his bones to align itself
with Venus & the Dog Star.

Some lodestone pulled him
to Banjo's show band on the highway
till Baltimore hexed him: a train
ticket & a telegram said a jealous
lover stabbed his father to death.
He followed a spectral cologne
till he was back with Hootie,
till that joke about chickens
hit by a car swelled into legend.
Now, he was ready to squeeze
elevenths, thirteenths,
every silent grace note
of blood into each dream
he dared to play.

III

Purple dress. Midnight-blue.
Dime-store floral print
blouse draped over a Botticellian
pose. Tangerine. He could blow
insinuation. A train whistle
in the distance, gun shot
through the ceiling, a wood warbler
back in the Ozarks at Lake
Taneycomo, he'd harmonize
them all. Celt dealing in coal
on the edge of swing. Blue
dress. Carmine. Yellow sapsucker,
bodacious "zoot suit with the reet
pleats" & shim sham shimmy.

Lime-green skirt. Black silk
petticoat. Velveteen masterpiece &
mindreader twirling like a spotlight
on the dance floor. Yardbird
could blow a woman's strut
across the room. "Alice in
Blue" & "The Lady in Red"
pushed moans through brass.
Mink-collared cashmere & pillbox.
Georgia peach. Pearlized façade
& foxtrot. Vermillion dress. High
heels clicking like a high hat.
Black-beaded flapper. Blue satin.
Yardbird, he'd blow pain & glitter.

IV

Moving eastward to the Deep
South with Jay McShann,
on trains whistling into dogwood
& pine, past shadows dragging balls
& chains, Bird landed in jail
in Jackson for lallygagging
on the front porch of a boardinghouse
with the lights on. For two days
he fingered a phantom alto
till "What Price Love" spoke
through metal & fluted bone.
The band roared through the
scent of mayhaw & muscadine,
back into Chicago & Detroit.

When the truckload of horns
& drums rolled into Manhattan,
Bird slid behind the wheel.
The three-car caravan
followed, looping Central Park
till a mounted policeman
brandished his handcuffs.
Days later, after moving into the Woodside,
after a battery of cutting contests,
Ben Webster heard them & ran downtown
to Fifty-second Street & said
they were kicking in the devil's door
& putting the night back
together up at the Savoy.

V

Maybe it was a day like today.
We sat in Washington Square Park
sipping wine from a Dixie cup
when Bird glimpsed Anatole
Broyard walking past & said,
"He's one of us, but he doesn't
want to admit he's one of us."
Maybe it was only guesswork
contorted into breath. We sat
staring after Anatole until he
disappeared down Waverly Place.
Bird took a sip, shook his head,
& said, "Now, that guy chases
heartbreak more than I do."

Maybe it was a day like today.
We were over at Max's house
as Bird talked Lenny
before Bruce was heard of,
telling a story about a club owner's
parrot squawking the magic word.
Maybe it was sunny or cloudy
with our tears, like other days
when Max's mama slid her key
into the front-door lock. Bird
would jump up, grab the Bible
& start thumbing through pages,
& Mrs. Roach would say, "Why
aren't you all more like Charlie?"

VI

If you favor your left
hand over the right, one
turns into Abel & the other
into Cain. Now, you
take Ikey, Charlie's half-brother
by an Italian woman, their father
would take him from friend
to friend, saying, "He's got good
hair." Is this why Charlie
would hide under his bed & play
dead till his mother kissed him
awake? No wonder he lived
like a floating rib
in a howl whispered through brass.

Always on the move, Charlie
traversed the heart's nine rings
from the Ozarks to le Boeuf
sur le Toit in Montmartre.
Though he never persuaded himself
to stay overseas, his first day
in Stockholm glowed among fallen
shadows. Always on some no-man's
land, he'd close his eyes
& fly to that cluster of Swedes
as he spoke of his favorite artist:
"Heifetz cried through his violin."
Charlie could be two places at once,
always arm-wrestling himself in the dark.

VII

Like a black cockatoo
clinging to a stormy branch
with its shiny head rocking
between paradise & hell,
that's how Yardbird
listened. He'd go inside
a song with enough irony
to break the devil's heart.
Listening with his whole body,
he'd enter the liquid machine
of cow bells & vibes,
of congas & timbales,
& when he'd raise his alto
a tropic sun beamed into the club.

Machito & his Afro-Cuban
Orchestra peppered the night
till Yardbird left ash in the bell
of his horn. He swore Africa
swelled up through the soles
of his feet, that a Latin beat
would start like the distant
knocking of tiny rods & pistons
till he found himself mamboing.
He must've known this is
the same feeling that drives
sap through mango leaves,
up into the fruit's sweet
flesh & stony pit.

VIII

He was naked,
wearing nothing but sky-
blue socks in the lobby
of the Civic Hotel in Little Tokyo,
begging for a quarter
to make a phone call. The Chinese
manager led him back to his room,
but minutes later a whiff of smoke
trailed him down the staircase.
This was how six yellow pills
sobered him up for a recording
session. He was naked, & now
as firemen extinguished the bed
cops wrestled him into a straitjacket.

Camarillo's oceanic sky opened
over his head for sixteen months
when the judge's makeshift bench
rolled away from his cell door.
Eucalyptus trees guarded this
dream time. Yardbird loved
working his hands into the soil
till heads of lettuce grew round
& fat as the promises he made
to himself, lovers, & friends.
Saturday nights he'd blow
a C-melody sax so hard
he'd gaze into eyes of the other patients
to face a naked mirror again.

IX

I can see him, a small boy
clutching a hairbrush.
This is 852 Freeman
Street, just after his father
took off on the Pullman line
with a porter's jacket
flapping like a white flag.
A few years later, he's astride
a palomino on Oliver Street
where a potbellied stove
glowed red-hot as a nightclub
down the block. Rudee Vallee
& late nights on Twelfth
haven't marked him yet.

When I think of Bird, bad
luck hasn't seethed into his body,
& Kansas City isn't Tom's
Town. This is before the silver
Conn bought on time, before Rebecca's
mother rented the second-floor,
before prophecies written on his back
at the Subway Club by Buster & Prez
on "Body & Soul," long before
Jo Jones threw those cymbals
at his feet, before Benzedrine
capsules in rotgut & the needle's
first bite, before he was bittersweet
as April, when he was still Addie's boy.

X

My darling. My daughter's death
surprised me more than it did you.
Don't fulfill funeral proceeding until
I get there. I shall be the first
one to walk into our chapel.
Forgive me for not being there
with you while you are at
the hospital. Yours most sincerely,
your husband, Charlie Parker.
Now, don't say you can't hear
Bird crying inside these words
from L.A. to New York,
trying to ease Chan's pain,
trying to save himself.

My daughter is dead.
I will be there as quick
as I can. My name is Bird.
It is very nice to be out here.
I am coming in right away.
Take it easy. Let me be the first
one to approach you. I am
your husband. Sincerely,
Charlie Parker. Now, don't
say we can't already hear
those telegraph keys playing Bartok
till the mockingbird loses its tongue,
already playing Pree's funeral song
from the City of Angels.

XI

I believe a bohemian girl
took me to Barrow Street
to one of those dress-up parties
where nobody's feet touched
the floor. I know it was months
after they barred Bird
from Birdland. Months
after he drank iodine,
trying to devour one hundred
black roses. Ted Joans
& Basheer also lived there,
sleeping three in a bed
to keep warm. A woman dusted
a powdered mask on Bird's face.

I remember he couldn't stop
talking about Dali & Beethoven,
couldn't stop counting up gigs
as if tallying losses: the Argyle . . .
Bar de Duc . . . the Bee Hive . . .
Chanticleer . . . Club de Lisa . . .
El Grotto Room . . . Greenleaf Gardens . . .
Hi De Ho . . . Jubilee Junction . . .
Le Club Downbeat . . . Lucille's Band Box . . .
The Open Door . . . St. Nick's . . . Storyville.
I remember some hepcat talking about
vaccinated bread, & then Bird began
cussing out someone inside his head
called Moose the Mooch. I remember.

XII

Bird was a pushover, a soft
touch for strings, for the low
& the high, for sonorous catgut
& the low-down plucked ecstasy
of garter belts. He loved
strings. A medley of nerve endings
ran through every earth color: sky
to loam, rainbow to backbone
strung like a harp & cello.
But he never wrung true blues
out of those strings, couldn't
weave the vibrato of syncopated
brass & ghosts
till some naked thing cried out.

Double-hearted instruments breathed
beneath light wood, but no real flesh
& blood moaned into that unbruised
surrender. Did he think Edgard
Varese & Stefan Wolpe could help
heal the track marks crisscrossing
veins that worked their way back
up the Nile & down the Tigris?
Stravinsky & Prokofiev. Bird
loved strings. Each loveknot
& chord stitched a dream to scar
tissue. But he knew if he plucked
the wrong one too hard, someday a nightmare
would break & fall into his hands.

XIII

They asked questions so hard
they tried to hook the heart
& yank it through the mouth.
I smiled. They shifted
their feet & stood there
with hats in hands, hurting
for headlines: *Baroness Pannonica* . . .
I told them how I met my husband
at Le Touquet airport, about decoding
for De Gaulle, about my coming-out ball.
I said I heard a thunderclap,
but they didn't want to hear
how Charlie died laughing
at jugglers on the Dorsey show.

The Stanhope buzzed with innuendo.
Yes, they had him with a needle
in his arm dead in my bathroom.
They loved to hear me say that
he was so sick he refused a shot
of gin. I told them his body
arrived at Bellevue five hours
later, tagged John Parker.
I told them how I wandered
around the Village in circles,
running into his old friends,
that a cry held down my tongue
till I found Chan, but they only
wanted us nude in bed together.

XIV

They wanted to hold his Selmer,
to put lips to the mouthpiece,
to have their pictures snapped
beneath *Bird Lives! Bird Lives!*
Scrawled across Village walls
& subway trains. Three women
sang over his body, but no one read
The Rubaiyat of Omar Khayyam
aloud. Two swore he never said
"Please don't let them bury me
in Kansas City." Everyone
has a Bird story. Someone
said he wished for the words
Bird recited for midnight fixes.

Someone spoke about a letter
in *Down Beat* from a G.I.
in Korea who stole back
a recording of "Bird in Paradise"
from a dead Chinese soldier's hand.
Someone counted the letters in his name
& broke the bagman's bank. Maybe
there's something to all this
talk about seeing a graven image
of Bird in Buddha & the Sphinx.
Although half of the root's gone,
heavy with phantom limbs, French
flowers engraved into his horn
bloom into the after-hours.

On the Corner

PHILIP LEVINE

Standing on the corner
until Tatum passed
blind as the sea,
heavy, tottering
on the arm of the young
bass player, and they
both talking
Jackie Robinson.
It was cold, late,
and the Flame Show Bar
was crashing
for the night, even
Johnny Ray
calling it quits.
Tatum said, Can't
believe how fast
he is to first. Wait'll
you see Mays
the bass player said.
Women in white furs
spilled out of the bars
and trickled toward
the parking lot. Now
it could rain, coming
straight down. The man
in the brown hat
never turned his head up.
The gutters swirled
their heavy waters,
the streets reflected
the sky, which was
nothing. Tatum

stamped on toward
the Bland Hotel, a wet
newspaper stuck
to his shoe, his mouth
open, his vest
drawn and darkening.
I can't hardly wait, he said.

Mingus at the Showplace

WILLIAM MATTHEWS

I was miserable, of course, for I was seventeen,
and so I swung into action and wrote a poem,

and it was miserable, for that was how I thought
poetry worked: you digested experience and shat

literature. It was 1960 at The Showplace, long since
defunct, on West 4th St., and I sat at the bar,

casting beer money from a thin reel of ones,
the kid in the city, big ears like a puppy.

And I knew Mingus was a genius. I knew two
other things but they were wrong, as it happened.

So I made him look at the poem.
"There's a lot of that going around," he said,

and Sweet Baby Jesus he was right. He laughed
amiably. He didn't look as if he thought

bad poems were dangerous, the way some poets do.
If they were baseball executives they'd plot

to destroy sandlots everywhere so that the game
could be saved from children. Of course later

that night he fired his pianist in mid-number
and flurried him from the stand.

"We've suffered a diminuendo in personnel,"
he explained, and the band played on.

Mingus at the Half Note

William Matthews

Two dozen bars or so into "Better Get It
in Your Soul," the band mossy with sweat,
May 1960 at The Half Note, the rain
on the black streets outside
dusted here and there by the pale pollen
of the streetlights. Blue wreaths
of smoke, the excited calm
of the hop in congregation, the long
night before us like a view and Danny
Richmond so strung out the drums
fizz and seethe. "Ho, hole, hode it,"
Mingus shouts, and the band clatters
to fraught silence. There's a twinge
in the pianist's shoulder, but this time
Mingus focuses like a nozzle
his surge of imprecations on a sleek
black man bent chattering across
a table to his lavish date:
"This is your heritage and if you
don' wanna listen, then you got
someplace else you'd better be."
The poor jerk takes a few beats
to realize he'll have to leave
while we all watch before another
note gets played. He glowers dimly
at Mingus, like throwing a rock
at a cliff, then offers his date
a disdained arm, and they leave in single
file (she's first) and don't
look back, nor at each other.

"Don't let me constrain you revelers,"
Mingus says, and then, tamed by his own rage
for now, he kick-starts the band:
"One, two, one two three four."

Mingus in Diaspora

WILLIAM MATTHEWS

You could say, I suppose, that he ate his way out,
like the prisoner who starts a tunnel with a spoon,
or you could say he was one in whom nothing was lost,
who took it all in, or that he was big as a bus.

He would say, and he did, in one of those blurred
melismatic slaloms his sentences ran—for all
the music was in his speech: swift switches of tempo,
stop-time, double time (he could *talk* in 6/8),

"I just ruined my body." And there, Exhibit A,
it stood, that Parthenon of fat, the tenant voice
lifted, as we say, since words are a weight, and music.
Silence is lighter than air, for the air we know

rises but to the edge of the atmosphere.
You have to pick up The Bass, as Mingus called
his, with audible capitals, and think of the slow years
the wood spent as a tree, which might well have been

enough for wood, and think of the skill the bassmaker
carried without great thought of it from home
to the shop and back for decades, and know
what bassists before you have played, and know

how much of this is stored in The Bass like energy
in a spring and know how much you must coax out.
How easy it would be, instead, to pull a sword
from a stone. But what's inside the bass wants out,

the way one day you will. Religious stories are rich
in symmetry. You must release as much of this hoard
as you can, little by little, in perfect time,
as the work of the body becomes a body of work.

Mingus in Shadow

William Matthews

What you see in his face in the last
photograph, when ALS had whittled
his body to fit a wheelchair, is how much
stark work it took to fend death off, and fail.
The famous rage got eaten cell by cell.

His eyes are drawn to slits against the glare
of the blanched landscape. The day he died,
the story goes, a swash of dead whales
washed up on the Baja beach. Great nature grieved
for him, the story means, but it was great

nature that skewed his cells and siphoned
his force and melted his fat like tallow
and beached him in a wheelchair under
a sombrero. It was human nature,
tiny nature, to take the photograph,

to fuss with the aperture and speed, to let
in the right blare of light just long enough
to etch pale Mingus to the negative.
In the small, memorial world of that
negative, he's all the light there is.

Bmp Bmp

for James McGarrell

WILLIAM MATTHEWS

Lugubriously enough they're playing
Yes We Have No Bananas at deadpan
half-tempo, and Bechet's beginning
to climb like a fakir's snake,
as if that boulevard-broad vibrato
of his could claim space in the air,
out of the low register. Here comes
a spurious growl from the trombone,
and here comes a flutter of tourist
barrelhouse from the pianist's left hand.
Life is fun when you're good at something
good. Soon they'll do the *Tin Roof Blues*
and use their 246 years
of habit and convention hard.
Now they're headed out and everyone
stops to let Bechet inveigle his way
through eight bars unaccompanied
and then they'll doo dah doo dah doo
bmp bmp. Bechet's in mid-surge as usual
by his first note, which he holds, wobbles
and then pinches off to a staccato spat
with the melody. For a moment this stupid,
lumpy and cynically composed little money-
magnet of a song is played poor and bare
as it is, then he begins to urge it out
from itself. First a shimmering gulp
from the tubular waters of the soprano sax,
in Bechet's mouth the most metallic
woodwind and the most fluid, and then

with that dank air and airborne tone
he punches three quarter-notes
that don't appear in the song but should.
From the last of them he seems to droop,
the way in World War II movies
planes leaving the decks of aircraft carriers
would dip off the lip, then catch the right
resistance from wet air and strain up,
except he's playing against the regular disasters
of the melody his love for flight and night's
need for gravity. And then he's up, loop
and slur and spiral, and a long, drifting note
at the top, from which, like a child decided
to come home before he's called, he begins to drift
back down, insouciant and exact, and ambles
in the door of the joyous and tacky chorus
just on time for the band to leave together,
headed for the *Tin Roof Blues.*

Blues for John Coltrane, Dead at 41

WILLIAM MATTHEWS

Although my house floats on a lawn
as plush as a starlet's body
and my sons sleep easily,
I think of death's salmon breath
leaping back up the saxophone
with its wet kiss.
Hearing him dead,
I feel it in my feet
as if the house were rocked
by waves from a soundless speedboat
planing by, full throttle.

A Riff for Sidney Bechet

Stanley Moss

That night in Florence,
forty-five years ago,
I heard him play
like "honey on a razor,"
he could get maple syrup
out of a white pine,
out of a sycamore,
out of an old copper beech.
I remember that summer
Michelangelo's marble
naked woman's breasts,
reclining Dawn's nipples—
exactly like the flesh I ached for.
How could Dawn behind her clouds hurt me?
The sunrise bitch was never mine.
He brought her down. In twelve bars of burnt sugar,
she was his if he wanted her.

The Day Lady Died

Frank O'Hara

It is 12:20 in New York a Friday
three days after Bastille day, yes
it is 1959 and I go get a shoeshine
because I will get off the 4:19 in Easthampton
at 7:15 and then go straight to dinner
and I don't know the people who will feed me

I walk up the muggy street beginning to sun
and have a hamburger and a malted and buy
an ugly NEW WORLD WRITING to see what the poets
in Ghana are doing these days
                                        I go on to the bank
and Miss Stillwagon (first name Linda I once heard)
doesn't even look up my balance for once in her life
and in the GOLDEN GRIFFIN I get a little Verlaine
for Patsy with drawings by Bonnard although I do
think of Hesiod, trans. Richmond Lattimore or
Brendan Behan's new play or *Le Balcon* or *Les Nègres*
of Genet, but I don't, I stick with Verlaine
after practically going to sleep with quandariness

and for Mike I just stroll into the PARK LANE
Liquor Store and ask for a bottle of Strega and
then I go back where I came from to 6th Avenue
and the tobacconist in the Ziegfeld Theatre and
casually ask for a carton of Gauloises and a carton
of Picayunes, and a NEW YORK POST with her face on it

and I am sweating a lot by now and thinking of
leaning on the john door in the 5 SPOT
while she whispered a song along the keyboard
to Mal Waldron and everyone and I stopped breathing

Bunk Johnson Blowing

in memory of Leadbelly and his house on 59th Street

MURIEL RUKEYSER

They found him in the fields and called him back to music.
Can't, he said, my teeth are gone.   They brought him teeth.

Bunk Johnson's trumpet on a California
early May evening, calling me to
breath of . . .
up those stairs . . .
calling me to
look into
the face of that
trumpet
experience
and past it
his eyes

Jim and Rita beside me. We drank it. Jim had just come back
from Sacramento the houses made of piano boxes the bar without
a sign and the Mexicans drinking we drank the trumpet music
and drank that black park moonlit beneath the willow trees,
Bunk Johnson blowing all night out of that full moon.
Two-towered church. Rita listening to it, all night
music! said, I'm supposed to, despise them.
Tears streaming down her face. Said, don't tell my ancestors.

We three slid down that San Francisco hill.

A Poem for Ella Fitzgerald

Sonia Sanchez

when she came on the stage, this Ella
there were rumors of hurricanes and
over the rooftops of concert stages
the moon turned red in the sky,
it was Ella, Ella.
queen Ella had come
and words spilled out
leaving a trail of witnesses smiling
amen – amen – a woman – a woman.

she began
this three agéd woman
nightingales in her throat
and squads of horns came out
to greet her.

streams of violins and pianos
splashed their welcome
and our stained glass silences
our braided spaces
unraveled
opened up
said who's that coming?

who's that knocking at the door?
whose voice lingers on
that stage gone mad with
        perdido. Perdido. Perdido.
        I lost my heart in toledooooooo.

whose voice is climbing
up this morning chimney
smoking with life

carrying her basket of words
> *a tisket a tasket*
> *my little yellow*
> *basket—i wrote a*
> *letter to my mom and*
> *on the way i dropped it—*
> *was it red . . . no no no no*
> *was it green . . . no no no no*
> *was it blue . . . no no no no*
> *just a little yellow*

voice rescuing razor thin lyrics
from hopscotching dreams.

we first watched her navigating
an apollo stage amid high-stepping
yellow legs
we watched her watching us
shiny and pure woman
sugar and spice woman
her voice a nun's whisper
her voice pouring out
guitar thickened blues,
her voice a faraway horn
questioning the wind,
and she became Ella,
first lady of tongues
Ella cruising our veins
voice walking on water
crossed in prayer,
she became holy
a thousand sermons
concealed in her bones
as she raised them in a
symphonic shudder
carrying our sighs into
her bloodstream.

this voice, chasing the
morning waves,
this Ella-tonian voice soft
like four layers of lace.

> *When I die Ella*
> *tell the whole joint*
> *please, please, don't talk*
> *about me when I'm gone . . . .*

i remember waiting one nite for her appearance
audience impatient at the lateness
of musicians,
i remember it was april
and the flowers ran yellow
the sun downpoured yellow butterflies
and the day was yellow and silent
all of spring held us
in a single drop of blood.

when she appeared on stage
she became Nut arching over us
feet and hands placed on the stage
music flowing from her breasts
she swallowed the sun
sang confessions from the evening stars
made earth divulge her secrets
gave birth to skies in her song
remade the insistent air
and we became anointed found
inside her bop

> *bop bop dowa*
> *bop bop doowaaa*
> *bop bop dooooowaaa*

Lady. Lady. Lady.
be good. be good
to me.

to you.　　to us all
cuz we just some lonesome babes
in the woods
hey lady. sweetellalady
Lady. Lady. Lady. be gooooood
ELLA ELLA ELLALADY
　　be good
　　　　gooooood
　　　　　　gooooood . . .

Joe Louis and the Duke

NEIL SHEPARD

It was June 22, 1938, at the Savoy.
It was active duty and Hitler blackening
the Alps with the long shadows of *Ubermenschen*.
From Fort Lee, New Jersey, to the Harlem clubs was a bridge
or a tunnel away—a span across that black Hudson starred
with city lights, or a dark dig beneath the river lit with carbon
arcs—some transport across that dark, dividing water. A free pass
from the base, a barracks bus, and I was there, jazzed

up, one of the few white guys in the club, and felt it, but felt black
as any welt, felt bruised and leathered as any fighter.
Earlier, I'd sat in the cheap seats of Yankee Stadium, watching
The Fight, the impossible, the slow German, Max Schmeling, knocked
    down
by lightning-fast Joe Louis in the first and only round, knocked down
and out. Now I knew what was possible. Now my ears popped

with Duke Ellington on the bandstand, all that false nobility
for real, whether it was Count or Duke
or Lady Day—and I had seen them in satin
earlier that night, at The Fight, Duke and Cab Calloway,
and Tallulah Bankhead, all feathered and bannered
and royal blues and purples, and as Schmeling fell
to his knees, unable to rise again, the Bismarck sunk,
the Uboats swamped, Helmiss cried *Unmoglich!* (Impossible!)
and Tallulah jumped up and screamed to the Schmeling fans,
"I told you, you sons of bitches!"and waved her peacock
plumes in their faces, those magnificent fragile eyes!—

so that, back at the Savoy, I was hardly surprised
to see The Brown Bomber jaunt in
who had just fought Hitler and Hess and Goebbels and

the Super-Race, and had destroyed it
from the opening bell—the fight lasted only 2 minutes,
Schmeling threw only 2 punches, he went down twice, and all
the hateful binary combinations of good/evil, white/black, master/slave,
came crashing down with the 1-2 combinations off Joe's fists—
and the great white hope lay sprawled on the canvas
like a bloody swastika—and everybody turned

as the King, Joe Louis, with his entourage
dressed to the tuxedoed nines, but with his royal purple boxing robe
    and hood
still draped over his head, walked, skipped, double-stepped,
all footwork and combinations, left jab, right cross, uppercut, and up
came Duke's horns, up the drum roll, up the piano's segregated
white and black notes, the Duke pounding them together in wrist-
snapping arpeggios, smashing those separations with blue notes,
crossing over from black to white and white to black—and down
went that great white hope, that thing shadowing the Alps,
down and out.

The Last LP

NEIL SHEPARD

in my jazz collection was *Kind of Blue*,
snagged from a Woolworth's bin—
dental floss, hair brush, Harlequin
romance, floppy slippers, and old LPs—
all for under a buck! And I plucked up
from under a 3-pak of panties, Fruit
of the Loom, that blue-black album:

There was Miles moody against a black
background blowing his silver horn,
eyes lidded, nose flared, lips pursed
to educate the air with a pensive phrase—
no dazzle with a bright blast or field-holler.
No . . . Cool, muted, understated, and under-
stood: that silence hung at the edge

of all he did, shaped every note
blown into space and time,
ready to take back
any place the breath refused
to fill. And in tribute
to that silence, Miles added
his own: All that muted brooding

lacquered the black album cover,
shaded the names of the giants—
Adderly, Evans, Coltrane, Kelly—
not popped from the black
by a fine white font, but varnished,
yellowed, some half-diminished thing,
and one blue phrase enlarged, *Kind of Blue*—

and further down that remainder bin, beneath
the yoyos and tissues and miniature Army men,
I found *Crying in the Cheap Seats*, the first
book of my jazz-poetry teacher, Bill
Tremblay. Impossible!—that same man
who had turned me on to Miles
and showed me the value of silence

when the game was rigged, and the rich
had so much, and the rest had less, unless—
if they listened, if they searched, they might find
fortune in the lowliest places, in the cheap
seats and remainder bins. Impossible!
That someone looking to floss his teeth
or brush her hair would find poetry

and jazz so dark, so common anybody
could put down that brush and cry
or else floss till the plaque burned
and the blood came and never stop
trying to clean out that silence
from the mouth that says *I'm Crying
in the Cheap Seats and I'm Kind of Blue.*

Don't Explain

Betsy Sholl

I just wanted to tell what I saw—
a brown river, the Raritan, sprinkled
with loosestrife petals, two cassette tapes
dangling from a high bridge, rippled & looping
like kite strings in the wind—but questions came in:
what was the music, snagged on dirty heads,
tossed from a car speeding over the bridge?
And since my father went to school here, could he
have stood at this culvert, stripping petals
into the river? Back then, did flocks of geese
trample the bank down to stark red clay?
Over the phone, Mother says *Oh sure, sure,*
to the brown water, to loosestrife and geese,
oh sure, the way she'd answer years ago
when I asked. Did they have cars back then? Trains?
Records? Later there were questions I didn't ask,
darker things—Did you know the same years you were
in school, Billie Holiday was scrubbing floors
in a whorehouse, playing Louis Armstrong
on an old Victrola? That would make Mother wince.
Ditto, if I asked, Were you ever so mad
you could've ripped out your favorite tape
and hurled it, so mad you half understand
the video—Woodstock redux—*Nine Inch Nails*
out-Hendrixing Hendrix, destroying something
they love *and* hate, yanking the keyboard
from its sockets, smashing guitar on amp,
again and again till only the drummer's
left, ducking hurled mikes—God.
I wanted to say wind unraveled those tapes

like an aria too beautiful to be heard,
so we have to imagine the song we'd play
till it wore out, then carry on inside us, wound
on spools of feeling that could spin it to mind any time.
That's what my dead father was to me—on a reel
for my comfort, better than life, till the night
I sat up reading in his own hand, letters
full of slurs, doors he wanted shut against
just about everyone. All night as I read,
my old tape slowed to the indecipherable
rumble of dead batteries and I ripped it out.
Though maybe it snagged on some undergirding
in my mind and still hangs, now limp, now billowing,
inaudible aftermath of rage, small lull
in the music, which lasts a while till something
shakes it up—the way two joggers saw me
on the culvert and just had to shout, *Don't jump,
ha ha*. Balance almost begs for that,
as if whatever made my father so intent
on closing doors, is what makes us now want
to hear the voices that were shut out, want
to rewind and play again the band hurling
instruments and mikes, dumping water buckets
on the crowd dancing in a lumbered frenzy,
young kids lost in the song, whipping their heads
so wet hair stings their faces, feeling part of
the muddy ground, not caring where the crowd
carries them as long as they're moving. And now
the static and screech—is this my father's lost voice
singing inside me, *The world's going down. And down—*
me singing back—*in order to rise?* Down
to where no one's shut out, down to the riverbank's
bare red clay, down to a voice like Holiday's,
that even on a bad tape made from old records,
sends her losses straight to the marrow—*Don't Explain,
Strange Fruit*—voice totally shot by the end,
as if the life couldn't be kept out,
the music couldn't keep itself from breaking.

Coltrane on Soprano

J.R. SOLONCHE

His
eyes are
so closed
they're op
en. From the
top of his he
ad, he sees the
music coming
at him eleven
notes at a time.
He must squee
ze them all thro
ugh this narrow
tongue flick of a
horn, this squeal
er, whiner, sopra
no, diva of a high
pitched saxophone.
Flurries of fingere
d-key-fingers indis
tinguishable from eac
h other, strike the honey
from the stone. O, blurry pain
and slurry sorrow suck the merci
ful marrow from this brass-gold bone.

McCoy's Hands at the Piano

LISA RUSS SPAAR

The left's a preposition and its noun,
laid out and down, built up and knocked over.
The right's a verb, both active
and being, a tight warped knot
that the fingers ravel and unravel.

Sometimes the left is a large tree trunk
with its elastic wind-tossed basket
of branches, and right is the birds
alighting there, weaving wreaths
and nests, then springing out in long, wild scales.
Or the right is leaves emerging,
sharp and real—leaves soughing
and singing, tearing away and screaming,
then stirring again, like a promise
in the left hand's shimmering glove of ice.

Think about the bird's body,
most whole then most apart
and extended over the invisible.
How its body abandons itself
to fall from air to earth,
collapsing above the branch, then
miraculously erect and perfectly formed
among the leaves of the tree,
whose limbs have ridden death a hundred times
to witness such transformations.

In Memoriam John Coltrane

MICHAEL STILLMAN

Listen to the coal
rolling, rolling through the cold
steady rain, wheel on

wheel, listen to the
turning of the wheels this night
black as coal dust, steel

on steel, listen to
these cars carry coal, listen
to the coal train roll.

Everything I Know About Jazz I Learned from Kenny G

MARCUS WICKER

All right, so not really. But the morning my pops found Kenny G lying on my nightstand I did learn a black father can and will enter a bedroom, only to find Kenny's CD, bad perm and all, cuddled too close to his eighth-grader's head. He will tiptoe from the room, turn the knob, then kick down the door in slippers. He'll drag the boy out of bed down two flights of stairs and toss him in front of a turntable. Listen here, he says. When you finish a record put it back in the sleeve and you better not scratch my shit.

I curl into a ball on our shag brown carpet and stare at his wall of LPs. Breakfast folds into lunch before I move an inch. When supper rolls around I am shaking. (This is how jazz begins. Out of hunger.) Getting to my feet, I pull a record from the shelf, read: *Black Talk!* Charles Earland. A needle collides into an empty groove and out sweats a funky wash of organ. It feels like the afro's voice, grinning from the record sleeve, has picked itself out in my gut.

Eric Dolphy squeals, leaps, and dives inside my abdomen. Roy Ayers kneads and vibrates my chest. Freddie Hubbard's wail could crack glass, my ribs. Pharoah Sanders shivers all over my face. Every wax-gash, nick, and hiss. Every cut. Every record pierces skin. I tap. I drone. I thrash. I scream. I listen to the *Freedom Now Suite.* It sounds like a welted voice wincing at the basement's night. A voice my father hears too.

He does not cave the basement door. He walks a dirge down those steps. Gently strokes my neck. Asks, Why are you crying, son? Dad, I ache. Because I've been down here forever.

But Bird

PAUL ZIMMER

Some things you should forget,
But Bird was something to believe in.
Autumn, '54, twenty, drafted,
Stationed near New York en route
To atomic tests in Nevada.
I taught myself to take
A train to Pennsylvania Station,
Walk up Seventh to 52nd Street,
Looking for music and legends.
One night I found the one
I wanted. Bird.

Five months later no one was brave
When the numbers ran out.
All equal—privates and colonels—
Down on our knees in the slits
As the voice counted backward
In the dark turning to light.

But "Charlie Parker" it said
On the Birdland marquee,
And I dug for the cover charge,
Sat down in the cheap seats.
He slumped in from the kitchen,
Powder blue serge and suedes.
No jive Bird, he blew crisp and clean,
Bringing each face in the crowd
Gleaming to the bell of his horn.
No fluffing, no wavering,
But soaring like on my old
Verve waxes back in Ohio.

Months later, down in the sand,
The bones in our fingers were
Suddenly x-rayed by the flash.
We moaned together in light
That entered everything,
Tried to become the earth itself
As the shock rolled toward us.

But Bird. I sat through three sets,
Missed the last train out,
Had to bunk in a roach pad,
Sleep in my uniform, almost AWOL.
But Bird was giving it all away,
One of his last great gifts,
And I was there with my
Rosy cheeks and swan neck,
Looking for something to believe in.

When the trench caved in it felt
Like death, but we clawed out,
Walked beneath the roiling, brutal cloud
To see the flattened houses,
Sheep and pigs blasted,
Ravens and rabbits blind,
Scrabbling in the grit and yucca.

But Bird. Remember Bird.
Five months later he was dead,
While I was down on my knees,
Wretched with fear in
The cinders of the desert.

Zimmer's Last Gig

PAUL ZIMMER

Listening to hard bop,
I stayed up all night
Just like good times.
I broke the old waxes
After I'd played them:
Out of Nowhere, Mohawk,
Star Eyes, Salt Peanuts,
Confirmation, one-by-one;
Bird, Monk, Bud, Klook, Diz,
All dead, all dead anyway,
As clay around my feet.

Years ago I wanted to
Take Wanda to Birdland,
Certain that the music
Would make her desire me,
That after a few sets
She would give in to
Rhythm and sophistication.
Then we could slip off
Into the wee hours with
Gin, chase, and maryjane,
Check into a downtown pad,
Do some fancy jitterbugging
Between the lilywhites.

But Wanda was no quail.
Bud could have passed
Out over the keys,
Bird could have shot
Up right on the stand,
Wanda would have missed

The legends. The band
Could have riffed
All night right by
Her ear, she never
Would have bounced.

The Duke Ellington Dream

PAUL ZIMMER

Of course Zimmer was late for the gig.
Duke was pissed and growling at the piano,
But Jeep, Brute, Rex, Cat, and Cootie
All moved down on the chairs
As Zimmer walked in with his tenor.
Everyone knew that the boss had arrived.

Duke slammed out the downbeat for Caravan
And Zimmer stood up to take his solo.
The whole joint suddenly started jiving,
Chicks came up to the bandstand
To hang their lovelies over the rail.
Duke was sweating but wouldn't smile
Through chorus after chorus after chorus.

It was the same with Satin Doll,
Do Nothing Till You Hear from Me,
Warm Valley, In a Sentimental Mood;
Zimmer blew them so they would stay played.

After the final set he packed
His horn and was heading out
When Duke came up and collared him.
"Zimmer," he said. "You most astonishing ofay!
You have shat upon my charts,
But I love you madly."

Singing Hellhounds:

Poems about Blues, Rock, & Pop

Blues for Robert Johnson

KIM ADDONIZIO

Give me a pint of whiskey with a broken seal
Give me one more hour with a broken feel
I can't sleep again and a black dog's on my trail

You're singing hellhound, crossroad, love in vain
You're singing, and the black sky is playing rain
You're stomping your feet, shaking the windowpane

I put my palm to the glass to get the cold
I drink the memories that scald
Drink to the loves that failed and failed

Look down into the river, I can see you there
Looking down into the blue light of a woman's hair
Saying to her *Baby, dark gon' catch me here*

You're buried in Mississippi under a stone
You're buried and still singing under the ground
And the blues fell mama's child,
Tore me all upside
Tore me all upside
Tore me all upside down

This Poem Wants to be a Rock
and Roll Song So Bad

Kim Addonizio

I'm gathered with my friends in my parents' garage
between the Toro mower and the washer,
practicing this poem at a deafening volume
while inhaling non-stick Pam from a Ziplock.

This poem captures the essence of today's youth,
a raunchy perfume called Fuck It,
excreted from the balls of a civet.

I like how those lines rhyme, just like in a song.
Axl Jimi Anne Sexton Erica Jong.

Let me tell you what this poem really wants:
it wants to make you slam dance and fist pump
until you crawl across a sticky club floor,
weeping with profound understanding

before you vomit in the Women's Room sink.
It wants you to listen to it over and over and over
so that thirty years from now

whatever wayward idiocy you were up to
will come back glazed with nostalgia—

Gee, remember wandering around the golf course
hallucinating in the middle of the night,
remember the security guard at your dad's work
finding us naked, and that guy with the knife
convinced we were insects from outer space,

those were the days, and that poem
was on everybody's car radio, in heavy rotation.
Let's go get the book again

and feel like we used to. Light some incense,
and a bunch of those vanilla votives.
Come over here and ravish me

while I recite this poem word for word,
including the awesome guitar solo
I can play with this beautiful instrument
made of nothing but air.

When Joe Filisko Plays the Blues

KIM ADDONIZIO

cotton claps & shouts in every Georgia field
& the hounds are set loose to run down the fox

they will forever never catch.
He can play a front porch on a rundown shack

where a man is singing his hurt
like pressing a thumb on a bruise,

probably it's shaped like a woman
or a few years in prison.

You can ride those blues all the way to Chicago
where the lake swallows snowmelt

& turns bitter with whiskey.
That's the kind of blues he plays.

The kind where a muddy cloud
looks like a train. The kind where a train

looks like a trip to Paris, & Paris
is a woman wearing nothing but jewels,

& you have to know her but never will.
Go back home, follow the high notes down.

Joe will take you all the way underground.
He'll fill your mouth with dirt

& convince you it's barbeque.
He'll lay those blues down on you.

If you meet the devil, tell him Filisko
sent you—he'll let you go.

If you meet an angel, hold on hard
& don't ever let her meet Joe.

Cigar Box Banjo

KIM ADDONIZIO

Blind Willie Johnson could coax
music from a single string. God plucked a rib
and found a woman. Concert aria
in the gypsy song, long groan
of orgasm in the first kiss, plastic bag
of heroin ripening in the poppy fields.
Right now, in a deep pocket of a politician's brain,
a bad idea is traveling along an axon
to make sure the future resembles a cobra
rather than an ocarina.
Still there's hope in every cartoon bib
above which a tiny, unfinished skull in
its beneficence dispenses a drooling grin.
The heart may be a trashy organ,
but when it plucks its shiny banjo
I see blue wings in the rain.

Open Mic

KIM ADDONIZIO

Everyone gets a microphone at birth
which is why everyone wails at first,
testing the mortal sound system.
Check one two, check check check
goes the bird mobile over the crib,
the miniature electric train,
the babbling, self-peeing doll which looks
at first like an infant and then
like your mother on her last Thanksgiving.
You feel like you've just stepped onstage
but here comes the wrap-it-up music,
the MC slitting his throat with his finger.
Next up is the fat chanteuse
who sounds like a gerbil
trying to produce an aria
while clenched in the mouth of a housecat.
Meanwhile, the wasted young
in one another's arms,
drinking endless pints of cheap beer
but mostly spilling it on each other
because to gesture is to slosh,
and the young are full of gestures,
Meet my friend and *Fuck off*
and *Let's go outside to get high,*
which they do, standing close together
in the doorway of the showroom
for discount medical equipment.
Meanwhile, the house band performs
for a few spastic dancers.
Your bar stool is bolted to the floor.
Your lonely, twitchy heart
lunges like a dog on a chain,

only dimly understanding the reason
it must exhaust itself
and then begin to howl,
though no one ever comes.

Understanding Tina Turner

TARA BETTS

Quiet girl found a voice mama could not quell
inside Nutbush City Limits. The baby
blasted beyond timid Annie Mae into Tina,
grind of muscle, hip, fierce calves
dominating heels into domesticity.

In the early music video era,
I soaked up her battered denim jacket,
leather mini-skirt, spiked wig and stilettos.
I'd throw my head back like her
rippling antennas of brown hair,
belting to no one in particular,
What's Love Got to Do with It?

Twenty years later, people joke
about Ike's fists granting Tina her name,
how she transitioned terror rooted
in spousal rhythm and blues to rock diva,
thunderdome warrior queen
with a mountain mansion overseas.

Hurts twang the womb
then escape into songs—like a man
who never holds you too close, too long,
trying to crush music within.

8 Fragments for Kurt Cobain

JIM CARROLL

1/

Genius is not a generous thing
In return it charges more interest than any
    amount of royalties can cover
And it resents fame
With bitter vengeance

Pills and powders only placate it awhile
Then it puts you in a place where the planet's
    poles reverse
Where the currents of electricity shift

Your Body becomes a magnet and pulls to it
    despair and rotten teeth,
Cheese whiz and guns

Whose triggers are shaped tenderly into a false
    lust
In timeless illusion

2/

The guitar claws kept tightening, I guess on your
    heart stem.
The loops of feedback and distortion, threaded
    right thru

Lucifer's wisdom teeth, and never stopped their
    reverberating
In your mind

And from the stage
All the faces out front seemed so hungry
With an unbearably wholesome misunderstanding

From where they sat, you seemed so far up there
High and live and diving

And instead you were swamp crawling
Down, deeper
Until you tasted the Earth's own blood
And chatted with the Buzzing-eyed insects that
    heroin breeds

3/

You should have talked more with the monkey
He's always willing to negotiate

I'm still paying him off . . .
The greater the money and fame
The slower the pendulum of fortune swings

Your will could have sped it up . . .
But you left that in a plane
Because it wouldn't pass customs and
    immigration

4/

Here's synchronicity for you:
Your music's tape was inside my walkman
When my best friend from summer camp
Called with the news about you

I listened them . . .
It was all there!
Your music kept cutting deeper and deeper valleys
    of sound
Less and less light
Until you hit solid rock
The drill bit broke
    and the valley became

A thin crevice, impassible in time,
As time itself stopped.

And the walls became cages of brilliant notes
Pressing in . . .
Pressure
That's how diamonds are made
And that's WHERE it sometimes all collapses
Down in on you

5/

Then I translated your muttered lyrics
And the phrases were curious:

Like "incognito libido"
And "Chalk Skin Bending"

The words kept getting smaller and smaller
Until
Separated from their music
Each letter spilled out into a cartridge
Which fit only in the barrel of a gun

6/

And you shoved the barrel in as far as possible
Because that's where the pain came from
That's where the demons were digging

The world outside was blank
Its every cause was just a continuation
Of another unsolved effect

7/

But Kurt . . .
Didn't the thought that you would never write
    another song
Another feverish line or riff
Make you think twice?
That's what I don't understand
Because it's kept me alive, above any wounds

8/

If only you hadn't swallowed yourself into a coma
    in Rome . . .
You could have gone to Florence
And looked into the eyes of Bellini or Rafael's
Portraits

Perhaps inside them
You could have found a threshold back to beauty's
    arms
Where it all began . . .

No matter that you felt betrayed by her

That is always the cost
As Frank said,
Of a young artist's remorseless passion

Which starts out as a kiss
And follows like a curse

The Blues

BILLY COLLINS

Much of what is said here
must be said twice,
a reminder that no one
takes an immediate interest in the pain of others.

Nobody will listen, it would seem,
if you simply admit
your baby left you early this morning
she didn't even stop to say good-bye.

But if you sing it again
with the help of the band
which will now lift you to a higher,
more ardent, and beseeching key,

people will not only listen,
they will shift to the sympathetic
edges of their chairs,
moved to such acute anticipation

by that chord and the delay that follows,
they will not be able to sleep
unless you release with one finger
a scream from the throat of your guitar

and turn your head back to the microphone
to let them know
you're a hard-hearted man
but that woman's sure going to make you cry.

In Bloom

STEPHEN CRAMER

The headlights arrowed into the gulf
&, as if four open windows
could never be enough,

the doors were all spread-eagled
for my first encounter—*collision*
might be a better word—with Nirvana:

the volume hiked up to distortion,
the heat, absurdly, still
cranking through all vents,

the haze of exhaust blooming
red through the brake lights,
because the shredded

vocal cords & the snarl of guitars
demanded their own weather.
In the hilltop parking lot

our front tires stopped just short
of the pavement's edge, & the planks
of headlights were strobed

by snow. School property,
but the night gave its cloaked
permission, & the music shot

through us like a dare, flooding
our chests with thrill
& risk. So we got running starts

& slammed our bodies onto the cheap
plastic, luging down the hill
toward the snow-mounded field. I forget

which of us first tried & failed
to surf. But it didn't matter—
once I dipped out of that horizon

of headlights, all was shadow,
& I rocketed down that hill, streaking
the few stars. My stomach

plunged through the sled,
& the world shifted from light
to dark to light as I alternately faced

the streetlamps far above & the deep
blues of the woods. The next year
a classmate would be taken—

taken: that's the word someone used,
as though he'd been lifted,
transported somewhere else—

after testing another slope.
Every town's got that one blind
turn, that one absurdly steep

hill, & this was both. The blitz
of adrenaline, the buzz of risk,
made a classmate try to drown

the new summer's monotony
in a motor's mechanical yawp.
His motorcycle's protracted snake

of a skid ended in a splay
of sparks, a truck's undercarriage.
We graduated from high

school the same day as the funeral.
There we stood in our ridiculous
gowns, silence feasting on our insides…

Not a shred of silence, that snowy
night when our tracks turned pure
ice, & a goalpost came into focus

at the last second. Someone squinted
& held up their hand to the car's
glaring lights & said *enough,*

let's bail. A buzzkill, though our only
buzz was speed. But bail we did.
So I remember the rush, the sting

of kicked up ice, the world turned
to an indigo blur, I remember
the music's rash abandon, its scowl,

that feel that something new
was happening, but most of all
I remember that hand held up

against all the damage & confusion
that would soon come. We all wiped
the snow from our bodies,

slammed the doors shut so that the car
became a box of sound, & we were all
inside that sound, amazed among springs

coiling through wasted leather,
& we turned toward our good
homes, our loving parents,

letting the music be the danger
we wanted to be, letting it continue
long after we had made ourselves stop.

Blackbottom

Toi Derricotte

When relatives came from out of town,
we would drive down to Blackbottom,
drive slowly down the congested main streets
    —Beubian and Hastings—
trapped in the mesh of Saturday night.
Freshly escaped, black middle class,
we snickered, and were proud;
the louder the streets, the prouder.
We laughed at the bright clothes of a prostitute,
a man sitting on a curb with a bottle in his hand.
We smelled barbecue cooking in dented washtubs,
    and our mouths watered.
As much as we wanted it we couldn't take the chance.
Rhythm and blues came from the windows, the throaty voice of
    a woman lost in the bass, in the drums, in the dirty down
    and out, the grind.
"I love to see a funeral, then I know it ain't mine."
We rolled our windows down so that the waves rolled over us
    like blood.
We hoped to pass invisibly, knowing on Monday we would
    return safely to our jobs, the post office and classroom.
We wanted our sufferings to be offered up as tender meat,
and our triumphs to be belted out in raucous song.
We had lost our voice in the suburbs, in Conant Gardens,
    where each brick house delineated a fence of silence;
we had lost the right to sing in the street and damn creation.
We returned to wash our hands of them,
to smell them
whose very existence
tore us down to the human.

Golden Oldie

RITA DOVE

I made it home early, only to get
Stalled in the driveway, swaying
At the wheel like a blind pianist caught in a tune
Meant for more than two hands playing.

The words were easy, crooned
By a young girl dying to feel alive, to discover
A pain majestic enough
To live by. I turned the air-conditioning off,

Leaned back to float on a film of sweat,
And listened to her sentiment:
Baby, where did our love go?—a lament
I greedily took in

Without a clue who my lover
Might be, or where to start looking.

Elvis's Twin Sister

CAROL ANN DUFFY

In the convent, y'all,
I tend the gardens,
watch things grow,
pray for the immortal soul
of rock 'n' roll.

They call me
Sister Presley here,
The Reverend Mother
digs the way I move my hips
just like my brother.

Gregorian chant
drifts out across the herbs,
Pascha nostrum immolatus est . . .
I wear a simple habit,
darkish hues,

a wimple with a novice-sewn
lace band, a rosary,
a chain of keys,
a pair of good and sturdy
blue suede shoes.

I think of it
as Graceland here,
a land of grace.
It puts my trademark slow lopsided smile
back on my face.

Lawdy.
I'm alive and well.
Long time since I walked
down Lonely Street
towards Heartbreak Hotel.

Wacko Jacko

He's a Very Sweet Down-to-Earth Person. A Lot Like Me.
—NAOMI CAMPBELL

THOMAS SAYERS ELLIS

The tabloids can't keep up with the surgeries,
the collecting, the animals, the shopping, all the candy wrappers
left like tabs everywhere,
so they make things up, things
hideous as hearsay, weird things, we believe:

> He and Janet
> are the same person.
> Diana Ross is his lover.
> They got married,
> and adopted Webster.

The bandaged, leftover nose—a rhino.
Lips, a tattoo, not a relief but a permanent painting of a kiss.
Predators, like female owls, in both eyes.
Mouth, a sharp snake. Snake, a pale cave.
The wildlife in the songs comes from

the same venom stubble comes from, testosterone, the body's land
       of seized porn.
Boy actors, special friends, alcohol to minors.

> The Elephant Man's bones,
> how much would something
> like that cost?

All he needs is rest, not the kind that immediately morphs
into a photo of him in an oxygen chamber,
     not his nightly media-funeral of insomnia.
Fame loves fame, but fame that hates fame spreads fame-hate.

Paparazzi like commas.
The tip of the nose is real, the tip of the nose is a prosthetic
but he can afford it: the expensive peace,
of speechless, bleached skin.
The only things entertaining has left for him to rule
      are all carnival and zoo-like,
but every fairy tale needs the daughter of a king
if it ever wants to become a Pop Empire, someone to say Never
(since his handlers won't) and someone to add grace,

      a little Priscilla,
      a princess,
      a Presley.

What to do with her after the make-up of damage control
      never wore off?
The record of their break-up, already broken
long before the awkward, televised kiss.
You know what they say about men with large, blotched hands
      and big blotched feet.
The only d she got was divorce.
Only certain types of touching allowed, a heaven they faked.
      You saw the video: skin glowing like a vow,
vow glowing like a lie, a smooth cry.

      "I love you."
      "I love you more.
      Blanket me."

First Party at Ken Kesey's with Hell's Angels

ALLEN GINSBERG

Cool black night thru redwoods
cars parked outside in shade
behind the gate, stars dim above
the ravine, a fire burning by the side
porch and a few tired souls hunched over
in black leather jackets. In the huge
wooden house, a yellow chandelier
at 3 A.M. the blast of loudspeakers
hi-fi Rolling Stones Ray Charles Beatles
Jumping Joe Jackson and twenty youths
dancing to the vibration thru the floor,
a little weed in the bathroom, girls in scarlet
tights, one muscular smooth skinned man
sweating dancing for hours, beer cans
bent littering the yard, a hanged man
sculpture dangling from a high creek branch,
children sleeping softly in their bedroom bunks.
And 4 police cars parked outside the painted
gate, red lights revolving in the leaves.

Cruising with the Beach Boys

DANA GIOIA

So strange to hear that song again tonight
Traveling on business in a rented car
Miles from anywhere I've been before.
And now a tune I haven't heard for years
Probably not since it last left the charts
Back in L.A. in 1969.
I can't believe I know the words by heart
And can't think of a girl to blame them on.

Every lovesick summer has its song,
And this one I pretended to despise,
But if I was alone when it came on,
I turned it up full-blast to sing along—
A primal scream in croaky baritone,
The notes all flat, the lyrics mostly slurred.
No wonder I spent so much time alone
Making the rounds in Dad's old Thunderbird.

Some nights I drove down to the beach to park
And walk along the railings of the pier.
The water down below was cold and dark,
The waves monotonous against the shore.
The darkness and the mist, the midnight sea,
The flickering lights reflected from the city—
A perfect setting for a boy like me,
The Cecil B. DeMille of my self-pity.

I thought by now I'd left those nights behind,
Lost like the girls that I could never get,

Gone with the years, junked with the old T-Bird.
But one old song, a stretch of empty road,
Can open up a door and let them fall
Tumbling like boxes from a dusty shelf,
Tightening my throat for no reason at all
Bringing on tears shed only for myself.

People Are Dropping Out of Our Lives

ALBERT GOLDBARTH

Joplin's voice, edged like a crack
in glass, breaks
out from the window and falls
two floors to the cold
campus night.
Across the empty street
one man stopped mid-step
listens attentively in the dim
verge of my peripheral vision.
Nameless, face
half-shadowed and form hunched
anonymous under windbreaker, he
and I balance
our sides of a city block.
Tenuous relationship.
We breathe. We form a spatial border.
In space we define, shape shifts
foot to foot and pocket to pocket.
As he exhales
a long black line of night
plumbs my throat for its measure.

Song:
hemorrhages up over Joplin's lips
and hits curbing. Litter:
cans, packs, crumpled cups
accept her flow and fill
beneath our footfalls like flasks
of invisible blood
from dead friends and lost lovers.

People are dropping out of our lives.
Pieces of constellation are missing.
And now, this man,
at his disappearance back
into flat shadow, now
as lamplight and real estate realign
to compensate for his physical absence,
now in that hole
attracting me across the street,
Joplin's words—like coal
never made it to diamond—
smoke the saffron-and-red-hot West Coast blues
from a black metallic brazier.

Nobody near. The house at my back,
my house, is all stoop and sill, all
exit. All panes have a shatter-pitch.
Nobody near. And only the rapid
passing flasher suddenly shines
fingerprints onto my blank window.
By that second of whorls, I know them,
angels of the night.
And, nobody near, and Linda playing
up and down my spine with her ghost hands,
I sing
past midnight with the choir:
Jimi Hendrix, Brian Jones, Jim Morrison,
and Janis. We sing,
the streets don't know what to do with it.
Linda's hands know all the notes,
a high one, a rising falsetto, the scales
tip in the sky and go for broke,
the star, the guitar, the shrieks
go higher, the hands go
capo up my neck.

Painkillers

THOM GUNN

The king of rock 'n' roll
grown pudgy, almost matronly,
Fatty in gold lamé,
mad king encircled
by a court of guards, suffering
delusions about assassination,
obsessed by guns, fearing
rivalry and revolt

popping his skin
with massive hits of painkiller

dying at forty-two.

What was the pain?
Pain had been the colours
of the bad boy with the sneer.

The story of pain, of separation,
was the divine comedy
he had translated
from black into white.

For white children too
the act of naming the pain
unsheathed
a keen joy at the heart of it.

Here they are still!
the disobedient
who keep a culture alive
by subverting it, turning

for example a subway
into a garden of graffiti.

But the puffy King
lived on, his painkillers
neutralizing, neutralizing,
until he became
ludicrous in performance.

The enthroned cannot revolt.
What was the pain
he needed to kill
if not the ultimate pain

of feeling no pain?

All Along the Watchtower

Tony Hoagland

I remember the pink, candy-colored lights
strung around an auditorium
shaped like an enormous ear
and a single, distant figure on a stage, gripping a guitar
that twisted like a serpent

trying to turn into a bird.
Sixteen, high on acid for the first time,
I flew above the crowd in a cross-legged position,
down corridors embroidered with my
dazzled neural matter. And all those arms,
adrift like wheatstalks in a storm, reached up
to touch the flank of something bright, and warm.

Talking 'bout my generation,
that got our instincts for living
from the lyrics of rock and roll
then blasted off into the future
with our eardrums full of scar tissue
and a ridiculous belief in good vibrations.

God of micrograms and decibels,
shirtless deity of drum solos and dance,
you fooled us good
over and over,

and we found out, again and again,
you couldn't hold a bolt of lightning
very long

you couldn't spend a lifetime
on the spire of a moment's exultation.

But the lit-up sign that says *Now Playing*
on the back wall of the brain
still leads me down
to that small illuminated stage,

and I swear that he's still standing there,
the skinny figure in a tanktop and old jeans—
a glittering guitar raised in his right hand
like a beacon on a psychedelic tower—,
I can hear the thunder and the reverb

while the band plays on,
I can taste the drugs and candy-colored light—
and the adolescent hunger for *more life more life more life*
still flashing, still calling out
like a warning, and a summons.

Are You Experienced?

TONY HOAGLAND

While Jimi Hendrix played "Purple Haze" onstage,
scaling his guitar like a black cat
up on a high-voltage, psychedelic fence,

I was in the parking lot of the rock festival,
trying to get away from the noise and
looking for my car because

I wanted to have something familiar
to throw up next to. The haze I was in
was actually ultraviolet, the murky lavender

of the pills I had swallowed
several hundred years before,
pills that had answered so many of my questions,

they might as well have been guided tours
of miniature castles and museums,
microscopic Sistine Chapels

with room for everyone inside.
But now something was backfiring,
and I was out on the perimeter of history,

gagging at the volume of raw data,
unable to recall the kind and color
of the car I owned,

and unable to guess, as I studied
the fresco of vomit on concrete,
that one day this moment

cleaned up and polished
would itself become
a kind of credential.

Without Music

MARIE HOWE

Only the car radio
driving from the drugstore to the restaurant to his apartment:

rock and roll, oldies but goodies,
and sometimes, softly, piano music

rising from the piano teacher's apartment on the first floor.

Most of it happened without music,
the clink of a spoon from the kitchen,

someone talking. Silence.

Somebody sleeping. Someone watching somebody sleep.

The Weary Blues

LANGSTON HUGHES

Droning a drowsy syncopated tune,
Rocking back and forth to a mellow croon,
    I heard a Negro play.
Down on Lenox Avenue the other night
By the pale dull pallor of an old gas light
    He did a lazy sway . . .
    He did a lazy sway . . .
To the tune o' those Weary Blues.
With his ebony hands on each ivory key
He made that poor piano moan with melody.
    O Blues!
Swaying to and fro on his rickety stool
He played that sad raggy tune like a musical fool.
    Sweet Blues!
Coming from a black man's soul.
    O Blues!
In a deep song voice with a melancholy tone
I heard that Negro sing, that old piano moan—
    "Ain't got nobody in all this world,
        Ain't got nobody but ma self.
        I's gwine to quit ma frownin'
        And put ma troubles on the shelf."

Thump, thump, thump, went his foot on the floor.
He played a few chords then he sang some more—
    "I got the Weary Blues
        And I can't be satisfied.
        Got the Weary Blues
        And can't be satisfied—
        I ain't happy no mo'
        And I wish that I had died."

And far into the night he crooned that tune.
The stars went out and so did the moon.
The singer stopped playing and went to bed
While the Weary Blues echoed through his head.
He slept like a rock or a man that's dead.

Chiffon

LYNDA HULL

Fever, down-right dirty sweat
  of a heat-wave in May turning everyone
    pure body. Back of knee, cleavage, each hidden

crease, nape of neck turning steam. Deep
  in last night's vast factory, the secret
    wheels that crank the blue machinery

of weather bestowed this sudden cool,
  the lake misting my morning walk, this
    vacant lot lavish with iris—saffron,

indigo, bearded and striated, a shock
  of lavender clouds among shattered brick
    like cumulus that sail the tops of highrises

clear evenings. Surprising as the iris garden
  I used to linger in, a girl distant from me
    now as a figure caught in green glass,

an oasis gleamed cool with oval plaques
  naming blooms Antoinette, My Blue Sunset,
    Festival Queen. This morning's iris frill

damp as fabulous gowns after dancing,
  those rummage sale evening gowns church ladies
    gave us another hot spring, 1967.

JoAnn who'd soon leave school, 14, pregnant,
    Valerie with her straightened bouffant hair.
        That endless rooftop season before the panic

and sizzle, the torched divided cities,
    they called me cousin on the light side.
        Camphorous, awash in rusty satin rosettes,

in organdy, chiffon, we'd practice
    girl-group radio hits—Martha Reeves
        but especially Supremes—JoAnn vamping

Diana, me and Valerie doing Flo and Mary's
    background moans, my blonde hair pinned
        beneath Jo's mother's Sunday wig.

The barest blue essence of Evening in Paris
    scented our arms. We perfected all the gestures,
        JoAnn's liquid hands sculpting air,

her fingers' graceful cupping, wrist turning,
    palm held flat, "Stop in the Name of Love,"
        pressing against the sky's livid contrails,

and landscape flagged with laundry, tangled
    aerials and billboards, the blackened
        railway bridges and factories ruinous

in their fumes. Small hand held against the flood
    of everything to come, the savage drifting years.
        I'm a lucky bitch. Engulfed in the decade's riotous

swells, that lovely gesture, the dress, plumage
    electrifying the fluid force of that young body.
        She was gang-raped later that year. The rest,

as they say, *is history*. History.
  When I go back I pore the phone book for names
    I'll never call. Peach Pavilion, Amethyst

Surprise. *Cousin on the light side.* Bend
  to these irises, their piercing ambrosial
    essence, the heart surprised, dark and bitter.

leadbelly: from sugarland

TYEHIMBA JESS

i push groan from gut, birthing a bloodlight into song, black
wave of texas roil rippin' cross cane field, heat mirage of field
holler syncopation, missin' link in a chain of gospel moans.
i stand here gideon sung, swinging sickle across cane where
i record the roadmap of pain, the way this confection bends
my back to a blood brown halo of motion, fills my grip with
blistered flesh, twists the sun into high noon heat from dawn
'til dusk. every day marches crushed and crippled into sin
sugared misery, bottom lands blessed with our sweltered hymn
curse.

i will tell you now and only once: only one way out. past
bloodhound and 20:20 gunshot, past swamp and gator tooth,
past lynch rope and lash: work these muthafuckas down.
outsweat and outshine even the hardest cracker smile, 'til they
think you death's scarecrow, 'til your grin tilts itself into their
daydreams, and your field holler moves the white chalked
nerve in them to wonder black, pauses, tell them the truth in
the lie they wanna hear: how you is more a man than they ever
wet dreamed to be, how your voice carves the bludgeon of
legend into a bent down sound that sways up earth. how one
black sound can tremble down these walls, how i'll pick up
each and every one of the twelve humming strings and make a
chorus of auction blocks and mama wails, how the midnight
special cries for me in a single streak of smoke headed north.

martha promise receives leadbelly, 1935

TYEHIMBA JESS

when your man comes home from prison,
when he comes back like the wound
and you are the stitch,
when he comes back with pennies in his pocket
and prayer fresh on his lips,
you got to wash him down first.

you got to have the wildweed and treebark boiled
and calmed, waiting for his skin like a shining baptism
back into what he was before gun barrels and bars
chewed their claim in his hide and spit him
stumbling backwards into screaming sunlight.

you got to scrub loose the jailtime fingersmears
from ashy skin, lather down the cuffmarks
from ankle and wrist, rinse solitary's stench loose
from his hair, scrape curse and confession
from the welted and the smooth,
the hard and the soft,
the furrowed and the lax.

you got to hold tight that shadrach's face
between your palms, take crease and lid
and lip and brow and rinse slow with river water,
and when he opens his eyes
you tell him calm and sure
how a woman birthed him
back whole again.

Booker Again

JULIE KANE

Booker is dead, but I still go
sit on the Maple Leaf patio

among the palmettos and elephant ears
to listen to music and drink a few beers

and check on the pink hibiscus tree
firing its blossoms like flares at sea

late in the year. Mention his name
and the bar help repeats the same

handful of stories—how he vomited on
the keys one night and Big John

had to clean it up with a bar rag;
how the dope arrived by White Fleet Cab;

how he stood up once with his pantseat shitty.
Beauty is truth, but truth is not pretty.

Never Land

YUSEF KOMUNYAKAA

I don't wish you were one
   of the Jackson Five
tonight, only you were

still inside yourself
   unchanged by the vampire
moonlight. So eager to

play The Other
   did you forget
Dracula was singled out

because of his dark hair
   & olive skin? After
you became your cover,

tabloid headlines
   grafted your name
to a blond boy's.

The personals bled
   through newsprint,
across your face. Victor

Frankenstein knew we must
   love our inventions. Now,
maybe skin will start to grow

over the lies & subtract
   everything that under-
mines nose & cheekbone.

You could tell us if
    loneliness is what
makes the sparrow sing.

Michael, don't care
    what the makeup
artist says, you know

your sperm will never
    reproduce that face
in the oval mirror.

Tu Do Street

Yusef Komunyakaa

Music divides the evening.
I close my eyes & can see
men drawing lines in the dust.
America pushes through the membrane
of mist & smoke, & I'm a small boy
again in Bogalusa. *White Only*
signs & Hank Snow. But tonight
I walk into a place where bar girls
fade like tropical birds. When
I order a beer, the mama-san
behind the counter acts as if she
can't understand, while her eyes
skirt each white face, as Hank Williams
calls from the psychedelic jukebox.
We have played Judas where
only machine-gun fire brings us
together. Down the street
black GIs hold to their turf also.
An off-limits sign pulls me
deeper into alleys, as I look
for a softness behind these voices
wounded by their beauty & war.
Back in the bush at Dak To
& Khe Sanh, we fought
the brothers of these women
we now run to hold in our arms.
There's more than a nation
inside us, as black & white
soldiers touch the same lovers
minutes apart, tasting

each other's breath,
without knowing these rooms
run into each other like tunnels
leading to the underworld.

Hanoi Hannah

YUSEF KOMUNYAKAA

Ray Charles! His voice
calls from waist-high grass,
& we duck behind gray sandbags.
"Hello, Soul Brothers. Yeah,
Georgia's also on my mind."
Flares bloom over the trees.
"Here's Hannah again.
Let's see if we can't
light her goddamn fuse
this time." Artillery
shells carve a white arc
against dusk. Her voice rises
from a hedgerow on our left.
"It's Saturday night in the States.
Guess what your woman's doing tonight.
I think I'll let Tina Turner
tell you, you homesick GIs."
Howitzers buck like a herd
of horses behind concertina.
"You know you're dead men,
don't you? You're dead
as King today in Memphis.
Boys, you're surrounded by
General Tran Do's division."
Her knife-edge song cuts
deep as a sniper's bullet.
"Soul Brothers, what you dying for?"
We lay down a white-klieg
trail of tracers. Phantom jets
fan out over the trees.

Artillery fire zeros in.
Her voice grows flesh
& we can see her falling
into words, a bleeding flower
no one knows the true name for.
"You're lousy shots, GIs."
Her laughter floats up
as though the airways are
buried under our feet.

Cher

DORIANNE LAUX

I wanted to be Cher, tall
as a glass of iced tea,
her bony shoulders draped
with a curtain of dark hair
that plunged straight down,
the cut tips brushing
her nonexistent butt.
I wanted to wear a lantern
for a hat, a cabbage, a piñata
and walk in thigh-high boots
with six-inch heels that buttoned
up the back. I wanted her
rouged cheek bones and her
throaty panache, her voice
of gravel and clover, the hokum
of her clothes: black fishnet
and pink pom-poms frilled
halter tops, fringed bells
and her thin strip of waist
with the bullet-hole navel.
Cher standing with her skinny arm
slung around Sonny's thick neck,
posing in front of the Eiffel Tower,
The Leaning Tower of Pisa,
The Great Wall of China,
The Crumbling Pyramids, smiling
for the camera with her crooked
teeth, hit-and-miss beauty, the sun
bouncing off the bump on her nose.
Give me back the old Cher,
the gangly, imperfect girl
before the shaving knife

took her, before they shoved
pillows in her tits, injected
the lumpy gel into her lips.
Take me back to the woman
I wanted to be, stalwart
and silly, smart as her lion
tamer's whip, my body a torch
stretched the length of the polished
piano, legs bent at the knee, hair
cascading down over Sonny's blunt
fingers as he pummeled the keys,
singing in a sloppy alto
the oldest, saddest songs.

Pearl

DORIANNE LAUX

She was nothing much, this plain-faced girl from Texas,
this moonfaced child who opened her mouth
to the gravel pit churning in her belly, acne-faced
daughter of Leadbelly, Bessie, Otis, and the booze-
filled moon, child of the honkytonk bar-talk crowd
who cackled like a bird of prey, velvet cape blown
open in the Monterey wind, ringed fingers fisted
at her throat, howling the slagheap up and out
into the sawdusted air. Barefaced, mouth warped
and wailing like giving birth, like being eaten alive
from the inside, or crooning like the first child
abandoned by God, trying to woo him back,
down on her knees and pleading for a second chance.
When she sang she danced a stand-in-place dance,
one foot stamping at that fire, that bed of coals;
one leg locked at the knee and quivering, the other
pumping its oil-rig rhythm, her bony hip jigging
so the beaded belt slapped her thigh.
Didn't she give it to us? So loud so hard so furious,
hurling heat-seeking balls of lightning
down the long human aisles, her voice crashing
into us—sonic booms to the heart—this little white girl
who showed us what it was like to die
for love, to jump right up and die for it night after
drumbeaten night, going down shrieking—hair
feathered, frayed, eyes glazed, addicted to the song—
a one-woman let me show you how it's done, how it is,
where it goes when you can't hold it in anymore.
Child of everything gone wrong, gone bad, gone down,
gone. Girl with the girlish breasts and woman hips,

thick-necked, sweat misting her upper lip, hooded eyes
raining a wild blue light, hands reaching out
to the ocean we made, all that anguish and longing
swelling and rising at her feet. Didn't she burn
herself up for us, shaking us alive? That child,
that girl, that rawboned woman, stranded
in a storm on a blackened stage like a house
on fire.

Decrescendo

LARRY LEVIS

If there is only one world, it is this one.

In my neighborhood, the ruby-helmeted woodpecker's line
Is all spondees, & totally formal as it tattoos
Its instinct & solitude into a high sycamore which keeps

Revising autumn until I will look out, &
Something final will be there: a branch in winter—not
Even a self-portrait. Just a thing.

Still, it is strange to live alone, to feel something
Rise up, out of the body, against all that is,
By law, falling & turning into the pointless beauty

Of calendars. Think of the one in the office closed
For forty-three summers in a novel by Faulkner, think
Of unlocking it, of ducking your head slightly
and going in. It is all pungent, & lost. Or

It is all like the doomed singers, Cooke & Redding,
Who raised their voices against the horns'
Implacable decrescendos, & knew exactly what they

Were doing, & what they were doing was dangerous.

The man on sax & the other on piano never had to argue
Their point, for their point was time itself; & all
That one wished to say, even to close friends,
One said beside that window: The trees turn; a woman

Passing on the street below turns up her collar against
The cold; &, if the music ends, the needle on the phonograph
Scrapes like someone raking leaves, briefly, across
A sidewalk, & no one alone is, particularly, special.

This is what musicians are for, to remind us of this, unless

Those singers die, one shot in a motel room
By a woman who made a mistake; & one dead
In a plane crash, an accident.

Which left a man on sax & another on piano
With no one to back up, &, hearing the news,
One sat with his horn in a basement in Palo Alto,
Letting its violence go all the way up, &
Annoying the neighbors until the police came,
And arrested him—who had, in fact, tears
In his eyes. And the other, a white studio
Musician from L.A., who went home & tried

To cleave the keyboard with his hands until
They bled, & his friends came, & called his wife,
And someone went out for bandages & more bourbon—

Hoping to fix up, a little, this world.

Body and Soul

Donna Masini

Michael leads us to the center of the dance floor
holding Kenny's hand, Kenny is dragging me and I
can't see Marie behind me, gripping my fingers.

The music (is this *music?*) is pumping, like it's coming
from inside, as if our hearts are the speakers,
desire urging through the wiry ventricles.

I am afraid my heart is going
to explode. The string of us strains, a chain
of kids playing rattlesnake, near the end

when the singing gets frantic, they're jumping, chanting,
eyes shut, shouting. Marie is shouting. We can't move
forward, back to the entrance

where the beautiful young man frisked us for Ecstasy.
We stop at a purple circle, a nervous halo
shaking on the floor. I can't see

eyes. Only teeth. I'm scared,
Marie shouts. Just dance, I motion.
White T-shirts writhe in the dark

like those cartoon ghosts that whoosh across a room,
the shirt moving when the body is gone, sucked
of desire. It's so loud our hearts hurt, but there's nothing

to follow. Someone's teeth curve up. Vampire white,
our smiles are frightening. Big in our faces. Hovering
over T-shirts. I am afraid

this is what heaven will be: body-shaped shades
bleached of their sins, the residual drifting
in space without faces. Who cares

how pure the soul is if you can't see
whose it is? If you can't say this
is Aunt Terri pinning up her hair, Jan

leaning forward to listen the way she does,
Judd unlatching his bicycle helmet. Goodness
to goodness, shirt to shirt, we're beyond

recognition. God, the Buddhists say,
is the breath inside the breath, but what is
dancing without seeing, without

flirting, wanting
someone's—anyone's—hand
to reach around, touch me.

Elegy for Bob Marley

WILLIAM MATTHEWS

In an elegy for a musician,
one talks a lot about music,
which is a way to think about time
instead of death or Marley,

and isn't poetry itself about time?
But death is about death and not time.
Surely the real fuel for elegy
is anger to be mortal.

No wonder Marley sang so often
of an ever-arriving future, that verb tense
invented by religion and political rage.
Soon come. Readiness is all,

and not enough. From the urinous
dust and sodden torpor
of Trenchtown, from the fruitpeels
and imprecations, from cunning,

from truculence, from the luck
to be alive, however, cruelly,
Marley made a brave music—
a rebel music, he called it,

though music calls us together,
however briefly—and a fortune.
One is supposed to praise the dead
in elegies for leaving us their songs,

though they had no choice; nor could
the dead bury the dead if we could pay
them to. This is something else we can't
control, another loss, which is, as someone

said in hope of consolation,
only temporary, though the same phrase
could be used of our lives and bodies
and all that we hope survives them.

The Deaf Dancing to Rock

LISEL MUELLER

The eardrums of the deaf are already broken; they like it loud. They dance away the pain of silence, of a world where people laugh and wince and smirk and burst into tears over words they don't understand. As they dance the world reaches out to them, from the floor, from the vibrating walls. Now they hear the ongoing drone of a star in its nearly endless fall through space; they hear seedlings break through the crust of the earth in split-second thumps, and in another part of the world, the thud of billions of leaves hitting the ground, apart and together, in the intricate rhythmic patterns we cannot hear. Their feet, knees, hips, enact the rhythms of the universe. Their waving arms signal the sea and pull its great waves ashore.

Comeback

PAUL MULDOON

We were introduced by Bruce
At the Stone Pony
All that concentrated juice
Standing room only
You were with some suit
From EMI or Sony
Who was so full of toot
He called for "Mony Mony"
You came back to the slum
The squat with Lars and Sammy
Then Lanois's green thumb
Grew us a golden Grammy
And then our double album
Hit a double whammy
When it reached number one
We reached for our swami

To make a comeback baby
A comeback don't you see
It's time to comeback baby
Come back baby to me

Then our master's voice
Told us it was cool
To park the Rolls-Royce
In the swimming pool
While our drugs of choice
Were run from Istanbul
Through a girl called Joyce
Whose real name was Mule

We loved the paparazzi flash
The paparazzi zoom
When we finished our stash
Of magic mushrooms
We'd pay in cash
For a kilo of Khartoum
And come back to trash
Another hotel room

And make a comeback baby
A comeback don't you see?
It's time to comeback baby
Come back baby to me

When we broke up we swore we'd never kiss and tell
Never speak to each other until hell
Freezes over or whatever hell does
When it's co-produced by Eno and Was
But *Behind the Music* and *Where Are They Now?*
Have pointed the way they've shown us how
To take a leaf from Plant and Page
And Fleetwood Mac and set the stage

For a comeback baby
A comeback don't you see?
It's time to comeback baby
Come back baby to me

We'd no sooner said farewell
Than it was time to reunite
A flame's likelier to swell
In a diminished light
For though we're a hard sell
What with the cellulite
We're still clear as a bell
We're still pretty tight

So let's remember the fans
As we fan the embers
And hit the Meadowlands
This coming September
When we take each other's hands
Baby let's remember
We're just another band
With only two surviving members

Making a comeback baby
From yet another rave
A comeback baby
A comeback from the grave

It's Never Too Late for Rock 'N' Roll

PAUL MULDOON

It may be too late to learn ancient Greek
Under a canopy of gnats
It may be too late to sail to Mozambique
With a psychotic cat
It may be too late to find a cure
Too late to save your soul

It may be too late to lose the heat
It may be too late to find your feet
It may be too late to draw a map
To the high desert of your heart
It may be too late to lose the poor
It's never too late for rock'n'roll

It may be too late to dance like Fred Astaire
Or Michael Jackson come to that
It may be too late to climb the stair
And find the key under your mat
It may be too late to think that you're
Never too late for rock'n'roll

We have to believe a couple of good thieves can still seize the day
We have to believe we can still clear the way
We have to believe we've found some common ground
We have to believe we have to believe
We can lose those last twenty pounds

Dream Team

PAUL MULDOON

We used to be partners
Along the winding road
Lennon and McCartney
Ratty and Mr. Toad
Wyatt Earp and Dodge
The girl who's kinda miffed
At the hodgepodge
The Three Kings brought as gifts
A dog and its manger
Strawberries and cream
Tonto and the Lone Ranger
We were a dream
We were a dream
We were a dream team

We used to be buddies
In our college days
The spine and the shudder
The Mets and Willie Mays
The petard on which we're hoist
Otis and the lift
The girder and the joist
Working the graveyard shift
History and Hegel
The mote and the beam
Lox and a bagel
We were a dream
We were a dream
We were a dream team

Until our efforts to tough
It out of the rough
Became the stuff of nightmare
Until we came to believe with Mae West
Saving love yields no interest
When you're such a messed-up pair

As used to be partners
In another life
Lennon and McCartney
Lot and his wife
The unconscious and Freud
Stella and Dean Swift
Staring into the void
Before they're set adrift
Freude and *Schaden*
Munch and *The Scream*
The Genie and Aladdin
We were a dream
We were a dream
We were a dream team

The Wailers in Estadio Nacional

Once Pinochet's Provisional Detention Center

Idra Novey

Before the concert, Ziggy Marley
says it again, *for the detained,*
tortured in this stadium—we play
for you.
                Two bare-chested boys
lift their joints and shout the name
of an uncle. Where I lie on a blanket,
everyone standing looks tall, hands
easy in their pockets— no way to tell
who was conceived under curfew
and who in exile, returned now
from East Berlin.
                Ziggy says
the first song's about democracy—
the lyrics in English, message
turned to cadence, to the grind and nick
of hips along the pocked wall, wheels
of the slow machine
                        that is a country.
The oval sky above the stadium
dims, dusky—the cut purple
of Santiago smog and summer,
of plums. He starts another song,
stating only, *this is not my father's.*

Waiting on Elvis, 1956

JOYCE CAROL OATES

This place up in Charlotte called Chuck's where I
used to waitress and who came in one night
but Elvis and some of his friends before his concert
at the Arena, I was twenty-six married but still
waiting tables and we got to joking around like you
do, and he was fingering the lace edge of my slip
where it showed below my hemline and I hadn't even
seen it and I slapped at him a little saying, You
sure are the one aren't you feeling my face burn but
he was the kind of boy even meanness turned sweet in
his mouth.

Smiled at me and said, Yeah honey I guess I sure am.

Cures

David Rivard

The part of the soul that doubts, again and again,
is scratchy as this song, "Mystery Train," where Elvis
relates some dark to himself. Even the light
in the living room seems sullen. We've turned the stereo
up loud, don't have to talk. After the latest argument,
trading blame is all that is left. After all that,
forgiveness? More punishment? Forgetting?
You curl, knees up, on the couch. Along your bare neck
the skin looks soft—shadows, the barrage
of falling brown hair, soft. I'm in the raggedy armchair,
and the music just washes through those questions,
then pours out the screen door. So this is what we do,
how we feel, each doubt a little larger
than desire, so that nothing
seems enough. And for a while,
ten minutes, I've stared at the album cover.
The face with the half-sneered, boyish charming smile
stares back from the floor. The words echo wall to wall,
then silence as one song ends and we wait for the next.
What do we think? His smoothness and raveling wail will cure us
of all this? These rockabilly blues
from the early Memphis days, a shy country kid
opening for Pee Wee Crayton at the Flamingo Club.
When all he cared about was shouting the next tune.

The next tune. But endings are truer
for all their need: a mansion outside town,
years of Seconal, gaudy stage suits. Ways to simplify
the hundred confusions screaming in the body,
to become a star, or something stranger. . . .

I'd like to go over and brush away the hair
from your face. All the questions,
all the night, as it strikes
the house like a train whistle. And after I get up,
cross the room, you and I aren't sorry
it leads to this kiss. Or to what it brings on,
a soothing that lasts only so long,
like stardom
in America, or now this silence between songs.

Bed Music

CHARLES SIMIC

Our love was new,
But our bedsprings were old.
On the floor below
They stopped eating
With their forks in the air,

While we went on
Playing our favorites:
"Shake it Baby,"
"Slow Boogie,"
"Shout, Sister, Shout."

That was the limit!
They called the cops.
"Did you bring some beer?"
We asked the law
As they broke down the door.

Monday, Monday

David Trinidad

Radio's reality when
the hits just keep
happening: "I want
to kiss like lovers
do . . ." Why is it
I've always mistaken
these lyrics for my
true feelings? The
disc jockey says it's
spring and instantly
I'm filled with such
joy! Is it possible
that I'm experiencing
nature for the first
time? In the morning
the sun wakes me
and I am genuinely
moved, almost happy
to be alive. For a
couple of weeks it'd
been getting a little
bit brighter every
day. I wasn't aware
of this change until
the morning I noticed
the angle at which
the light hit your
GQ calendar, fully
accentuating the aus-
tere features of this
month's male model, as
I sat in the kitchen,

in your maroon robe,
and waited for my tea
to cool. I was thinking
about my feelings, about
how much I loved the sun
when I was a child and
how I loved the dark
as well, how thrilling
it was to lie in bed
on windy nights and
listen to the sound of
bushes and branches being
thrashed about outside.

Actually, that's what
I was thinking while
you were making the tea.
I was staring at the
calendar, at the smoke
from the tip of my
cigarette as it drifted
in the sunlight toward
the open window, when
you set the steaming
fifties-style cup in
front of me. Was it
at this point that
my manner changed?
Your gesture reminded
me of innumerable
mornings spent with
my parents in the pink
kitchen of my childhood.
I remembered my mother,
how she always wore her
gaudy floral bathrobe
and shuffled about in
her bedroom slippers as

she dutifully served us
breakfast. My father
sat alone at one end
of the table, his stern
face all but hidden
behind the front page
of the *Los Angeles Times*.
They seldom spoke. I
felt the tension between
them, watched with sleep-
filled eyes as he gave
her the obligatory kiss
on the cheek, then
clicked his briefcase
shut and, without a word,
walked out the door.

As I was getting dressed,
you grabbed me, kissed
me on the lips, said
something romantic.
I left your apartment
feeling confused, got
on the freeway and
inched my way through
the bumper-to-bumper
traffic. I was confused
about sex, about the
unexpected ambivalence
which, the night before,
prompted my hesitancy
and nonchalant attitude:
"It's late," I said,
"Let's just sleep."
The cars ahead of me

wouldn't budge. I
turned on the radio and
started changing stations.
I was afraid I would
always be that anxious,
that self-obsessed, that
I might never be able
to handle a mature
relationship. Stuck on
the freeway like that,
I was tempted to get
into it, the pain and
the drama, but the mood
soon passed. (After
all, it *is* spring.)
At last, traffic picked
up and I enjoyed the
rest of the drive, kept
the radio on all
the way to work and
listened to all those
songs, though I finally
realized those songs
were no longer my feelings.

Record

KATRINA VANDENBERG

Late night July, Minnesota,
John asleep on the glassed-in porch,
Bob Dylan quiet on a cassette

you made from an album
I got rid of soon after
you died. Years later,

I regret giving up
your two boxes of vinyl,
which I loved. Surely

they were too awkward,
too easily broken
for people who loved music

the way we did. But tonight
I'm in the mood for ghosts,
for sounds we hated: pop,

scratch, hiss, the occasional
skip. The curtains balloon;
I've got a beer; I'm struck

by guilt, watching you
from a place ten years away,
kneeling and cleaning each

with a velvet brush before
and after, tucking them in
their sleeves. Understand,

I was still moving then.
The boxes were heavy.
If I had known

I would stop here
with a husband to help me
carry, and room—too late,

the college kids pick over
your black bones on Mass. Ave.,
we'll meet again some day

on the avenue but still,
I want to hear it,
the needle reaching the end

of a side and playing silence
until the arm gives up,
pulls away.

American Bandstand

MICHAEL WATERS

The boy rehearsing the Continental Stroll
before the mirror in his bedroom—
does he memorize the sweep of hair
tumbling across his eyes
when he spins once, then claps his hands?

Home from school in winter,
he studies the couples on television,
their melancholy largo,
how they glide together, then separate.
Such dancing makes him nervous—
so many hand motions to remember,
where to slide his feet, and
every girl in the gym staring at him.

That boy was familiar, twenty years ago,
saying hello to a loneliness
peculiar to the tender, the high-strung
lanterns suspended above the dance floor,
ousting shadows, leaving him
more alone, trapped in the spotlight.

The Peppermint Twist, The Bristol Stomp,
The Hully Gully are only memory,
but loneliness still dances
among the anxious ghosts of the heart,
preparing to stroll
down a line formed by teenagers
mouthing lyrics, clapping hands,
forever awkward,
each partner dreaming of grace.

The Burden Lifters

MICHAEL WATERS

At least you left me the green-gold
    dial of the radio
        sending forth its watery

light as I listened
    to the all-night talk
        shows till, bored with G

spots, vigilantes, the midnight
    madness at Crazy Eddie's,
        I tuned in the gospel

station, letting Willis Pittman
    and his Burden Lifters
        undo the damage of too

much talk—their harmonies
    soared above New York,
        held back the endless

babble of traffic, reduced
    the hubbub of static
        to a hush. In the back-

ground rose the sound
    of women weeping, trudging
        to the altar to be touched

by some euphoric preacher
   for the sake of the souls
      of their junk-ridden sons.

How many phone calls did I make,
   prayer aprons purchase
      from Reverend Ike, a host

of DJs spanning the seaboard,
   wanting someone to bless
      the hurt away, lift

my burden, let me groan,
   Lord, into the black
      telephone till dawn

eased down its light,
   gentle fingers upon
      my godforsaken shoulders?

Beauty in the World

Michael Waters

So much beauty in the world… trills Macy Gray
And the studio crew claps rhythmically
Into the mic
                clap clap clap clap clap clap clap
As though the response to beauty should be applause,
As in fact it was each summer evening in the '80s
At the outdoor café on the cliff on Ios
Where the rousing final movement of Dvořák
Was synced to the sun's declension
So that the orchestra crescendoed
Then abruptly ceased at the precise moment
The amaranthine disc of sun
Dissolved into the Aegean,
All of us burnt and stoned and giddy
As we burst into applause
Before nimbling the goat paths to hostels
Where we showered in anticipation
Of the modest debaucheries of night.
But it's the applause that stays with me
Rather than the ravers on holiday
In their sheer linens and seamless tans,
The applause and the beauty
That provoked it, the sunset
So elemental in that sparse landscape, the inexhaustible
Swyving of sun and sea, the hissing
We thought we heard below the cellos
And violas and tympani
Less the devil's beckoning tongue
Than the sizzle of skin, perversely
Pleasurable, more than enough
Sacrifice for our sins as we stared all day
At each other's bodies then entered them

Each night, that sibilant *pssst* louder
As flesh touched flesh in imitation
Of sun and sea, in homage to sun and sea,
To so much beauty in the world, O
Macy Gray, I'm clapping along right now
Stopped at the traffic light
Years and miles away from the island
Which still blazes in beauty without me,
Even at this hour when all the young fuckers
Who have followed my hoofprints
Sigh in their sleep
And the sun slips out of the sea
With no one watching, not one
Lost sylph searching for her sandal
Or ghost of shepherd
Or farmer on donkey to begin this day
With the joyful prayer of applause.

Ooh My Soul

—Little Richard

CHARLES HARPER WEBB

By night, ghosts roam Aunt Ermyn's
elm-shrouded, hundred-year-old home.
By day, my cousin Pete, just out of high school,
combs his duck-tail and keeps time
to records with his creaky rocking chair.
I'm in the hall, creating all-star teams
of baseball cards when, blaring
through Pete's open door, I hear . . .
war drums? Or is it a runaway train?
Keepa knockin' but you cain't come in,
some kind of preacher shrieks,
then squeals like tires around a curve.
Those chugging drums, smoking piano,
squawking duck-call saxophones
make me feel like an oil rig ready to blow.
I see wells pumping, teeter-totters bumping,
giant turtle-heads working out and in
as bronco riders wave tall hats in the air.
I see girls twirling, dresses swirling
high over their underwear,
guys doing splits, or inch-worming
across the floor.
                    It makes me want
to slam my head back and forth
like a paddle ball—to jump, shout, bang
my hands on walls, and flap them
in the air—to fall onto the ground
and writhe, flail, roar like Johnny Cerna
in his famous Kiddieland tantrum.
Keepa knockin' but you cain't come in,

the preacher howls. But I *am* in.
I'm in the living room, Bandstand on TV,
Dad ranting, "goddamn Congo beat!"
I'm in the back seat of his Ford
a decade later, learning what that beat
could be. I'm in my first band, hoarse
from screaming "Long Tall Sally."
I'm in my college dorm, trying to jam
that wild abandon into poems.
I'm in my car, heading for work,
when *Good Golly, Miss Molly!*
catapults out of my Blaupunkt stereo.
I'm walking into Pete's bedroom,
where I've never dared to go. Oh,
womp bompalumomp, a lomp bam boom!
I'm not thinking in words, but I know
I've spent my seven years rehearsing
how to feel this way. It's more exciting
than a touchdown any day, or a home run,
a gunfight, hurricane waves at Galveston,
a five-pound bass on a cane pole.
"What is that?" I ask Pete. He says,
"Rock-and-roll."

Nuh-Nuh-Nuh-Nuh-Nuh-Nuh-Nuh-Nuh-Nuh, Dah Dah Dah! Doesn't Look Like Much in Print

Charles Harper Webb

Hammered, though, on Led Zeppelin's bass and guitar,
didn't those sounds surge and shake like Linda in Mom's
Simca with the stuffing coming out? Weren't they my fists,
making a strawberry frappé out of Fred's mouth

(the double-crossing sack of scat)? Didn't they catch
the shimmering green-gold of dorado flipping,
flopping, flying, trying not to die after they slammed
my Deceiver, then ripped up the Sea of Cortez while Jesus,

my guide, coached me in speed-metal Spanglish?
Seguro que by God *si!* The shoe-sized, scrambling roach
that made Cecilia scream, the urinal ice that shrinks
in your hot stream—it's all in those staccato chords.

But does *staccato* say it? Sorry, not today.
Can words compete with "Meditation from *Thais*"?
No alliteratin' way. It's the best kiss you ever had,
the most beautiful bed-partner: squish of lips and brush

of thighs, mountain bluebirds in the trees, and butterflies—
painted ladies, red admirals, spicebush swallowtails,
but mourning cloaks too, because the kiss subsides,
the ladies die, ants gang-drag them away. Under

the beauty, there's that coyote's-caught-a-housecat squeal
that jerked you out onto your porch, dark churning in.
"Does Your Chewing Gum Lose Its Flavor on the Bedpost
Overnight?" isn't poetry, but when the banjo bangs

as Lonnie Donegan noses the tune—hey, it's leaping out
of bed for summer swimming and cartoons. It's thrash-
in-the-grass hilarious when you and your friends are wasted,
whacked-out, fecal-faced. It's vaulting off your pew,

high-stepping down the aisles, cold-cocking deacons
with collection plates. What good are whiff-of-pancake
words when you crave a steaming stack; a glimpse
of thigh, when you're starved for the whole girl? Forget

the IRS and idiot President; "Stars and Stripes Forever"
flaps me like a flag. I dump irony out of my duffel-bag,
and cry to think how many died in World War II
so Santa could bring me a hi-fi to play "Rave On"

and "Topsy II," every blood-cell banging its bongo
with Cozy Cole, every neuron igniting when Buddy sang,
"Uh weh heh heh heh hell . . . " No way in heh heh hell
can words say that, or tell how good it felt to jam

my sunburst Stratocaster in my crotch and hump like Hendrix
whanging "Little Miss Lover," wah-wah pedal plugged
into my spine, sound roaring out the way the world
roared out of God—plum trees, ferrets, the Appalachians

and Ganges, crabgrass and brown recluse spiders, Ford
Falcons and dudes named Buck and Fabian, chicks
named Tiffany and Krys, and winning the Big Fish Pool
on the Lindy Lou with a lingcod longer than I was tall at ten,

and no-handling my bike home from Natalie's after we kissed—
A WHUNK da ta WA ta, a WHUNKa whunk WHAA
flash-flooding out of me: Rock-Yahweh with a guitar I loved
so much that, when some crackhead robs my home,

it isn't my computer full of poems that I mourn, but that guitar—
the notes it still had left to play—the night when, bound
for a real job with a real salary, I tucked my love into its case,
and lugged the case, black as a coffin, off the stage.

Love Letter to Justin Timberlake

MARCUS WICKER

When I think of you
it is always of a small, locked room.
A principal's dark, full lips
pressed together in a smirk. A glare
from his fat, gold herringbone chain
burning tears in my eyes, my face
red as yours in direct sunlight. And
even as my voice shut down
that day, I knew ditching
to buy *NSYNC's CD
was worth more than
Prescriptive Speech class.
What I heard: four voices
harmonized in a plastic bottle.
Your falsetto, blowing the top off.
Michael Jackson
with no abusive boxer father
or snatched childhood.
Sam Cooke
sans German shepherds
stalking through his songs.
I've been watching James Brown
and Jackie Wilson make
pelvic fixation public domain
since I was old enough
to work a remote. And I have yet
to elude starched lines. How did you
learn to dance your way out of boxes?
Or did you
find it easy as breathing, like whistling
the national anthem?

Do you remember the Super Bowl?
How you tore Janet Jackson's breast
from her top?
I love you that way.
Her earth-brown bounty of flesh–
large, black nipple
pierced, wind chapped, hardened.
And you saying, Go ahead. Look.

Jerry Lee Lewis's Secret Marriage to Thirteen-Year-Old First Cousin Revealed During British Isles Tour, 1959. His Manager Speaks:

David Wojahn

Dumb career move, killer. The IRS is on your case,
Sending letters, agents. And you say it's just a bad luck streak?
Christ, she doesn't even menstruate!
My bookie'd give your pre-vert marriage eight weeks.
What do you talk about at night, or need I ask?
And get this through your stupid cracker skull:
Your little stunt's a felony in every state
But Arkansas. Get it? *Il-leg-al.*

So go ahead and play piano with your nose,
And tear your shirt off singing "High School Confidential."
But the Feds'll take the Cadillac and the clothes,
Leave you without a nose to pick. They play hardball.
They'll bleed you until every penny's spent.
Your ass is grass, and where's my ten percent?

Tattoo, Corazon: Ritchie Valens, 1959

DAVID WOJAHN

He has three singles on the charts and in
Six weeks will be dead,
                    the Piper Cub that also kills

Big Bopper, Buddy Holly and almost Dion,
Skidding to pieces in an Iowa field.

Easy to imagine premonitions—
That he wakes in night-sweats from dreams of falling—
But no.
          Harder to say he's seventeen
And buys, with cash, a house in West L.A.,

Where he's sprawled tonight, sculpting in his bedroom
A gift for his new wife. His left hand turns

The knife in circles on his right. Where thumb
And index finger meet, he cuts and squirms,

Replacing blood with ink. Cotton stops the flow.
She'll wake to heart shape,
                  circling TE AMO.

Elvis Moving a Small Cloud: The Desert Near Las Vegas, 1976

—after the painting by Susan Baker

David Wojahn

"Stop this motherfucking Limo," says the King,
And the Caddie, halting, raises fins of dust
Into a landscape made of creosote,
Lizards, dismembered tires. The King's been reading

Again. *Mind Over Matter—Yogic Texts*
On Spiritual Renewal by Doctor Krishna
Majunukta, a Guide on How To Tap the
Boundless Mental Powers of the Ancients.

Body-guards and hangers-on pile out.
His highness, shades off, scans the east horizon.
"Boys, today I'm gonna show you somethin'
You can tell your grandchildren about."

He aims his finger at Nevada's only cloud.
"Lo! Behold! Now watch that fucker *move!*"

Francis Ford Coppola and Anthropologist Interpreter Teaching Garteweinna Tribesmen to Sing "Light My Fire," Philippine Jungle, 1978

DAVID WOJAHN

It's done phonetically, of course, at great
Expense. Dr. Singh, the bull-horned anthropologist,

Struts with Francis on the peopled set, insists
On short hours for the warriors, who must hunt

Wild pig tomorrow, an annual ritual
That should not be disturbed.
                                    But integrity

Matters less to him than his large consulting fee.
Back in Manila, he will buy a Mercedes SL

And forget about the Leader's new doubleknits,
Leader's Number-Three-Wife
                                    snorting coke with Dennis Hopper,

Brando signing glossies for the witch doctor
To grind into aphrodisiacs.
                        CAW-MAWN   BAY-BE   LIGHT

MY FOY-OR they chant.
                        "What mean *Apocalypse Now*?" asks Leader.

Dr. Singh: "Mean: *everybody-die-together-here.*"

The Assassination of John Lennon as Depicted by the Madame Tussaud Wax Museum, Niagara Falls, Ontario, 1987

DAVID WOJAHN

Smuggled human hair from Mexico
Falls radiant around the waxy O

Of her scream. Shades on, leather coat and pants, Yoko
On her knees—like the famous Kent State photo

Where the girl can't shriek her boyfriend alive, her arms
Windmilling Ohio sky.
                                        A pump in John's chest heaves

To mimic death-throes. The blood is made of latex.
His glasses: broken on the plastic sidewalk.

A scowling David Chapman, his arms outstretched,
His pistol barrel spiraling fake smoke

In a siren's red wash, completes the composition,
And somewhere background music plays "Imagine"

Before the tableau darkens. We push a button
To renew the scream.
                                        The chest starts up again.

Homage to Blind Willie Johnson

David Wojahn

Past Phobos & Demos, past Mars & its gorges of fossil water,
Past the wheeling numberless moons of Jupiter,
Past asteroid, crater & absolute zero, past red gas thunderclaps

More massive than a dozen earths, celestial
Himalayas of ice, the bright coronal Saturn rings,
Past Neptune, Triton & storm-wracked Uranus,

Past spirochete comet head & the bleak realm
Of fallen sky gods, past darkling Pluto
Where sunlight is distant as a schoolroom

In the Alzheimer-riven midbrain of my grandfather,
Past color and conception, past sound wave
And the lavish carpal symmetries of gravity,

Past the Great Influenza of 1918 & the turbid
Bayous of East Texas seething cottonmouths, past
A training for salvation courtesy of a bottle of lye

Burned into his six-year-old eyes by his stepmother,
Raging at his Daddy's stray cat low down ways,
Past urinous shack & sharecropper cotton,

A cigar-box guitar, fashioned of catgut and willow wood,
Past Beaumont & flophouse & Blood of the Lamb,
Past Jim Crow & Pentecost & Nacogdoches, past the Full Gospel

Tabernacle African Reformed & street-corner preaching
On the matter of John the Revelator, beholding His Book
Of Seven Seals, & the bees making honey in the lion's head,

Past cylinder disk & quarter note, past undulating neon
& a primitive mike in a Dallas hotel, 3 December 1927,
A back-up band of foot stomp, & the engineer coughing,

Blind Willie Johnson is flying.
On the Voyager Spacecraft he is flying,
With a Brandenburg Concerto & Olivier

Intoning Hamlet, with the symbol for pi
He is flying, message in a bleeping whirring bottle
Hurled skyward for the delectation

Of extraterrestrials ten thousand years hence.
He is flying made of nothing but the otherworldly wail
Of "Dark was the Night, Cold was the Ground,"

Wherein a hymnbook cliché is transfigured
& the afterlife commences with glissando,
Bottleneck & string, then the fretwork slowing

As the prayer-wheel cry emerges. The lyrics,
Like this earthly boy, shed, replaced by feral moan.
Ah well, aaahhhh well, ah well ah well aaahhh well

Ah Lord. Our sorrows survive us, transfigured also.
Our sorrows lead us to the Promised Land.
Ah well, aahhh well. Bardo, Pleroma, Pearly Gate

& Shangri-la. Our sorrows pulse their sacred
Glossolalia up & down the strings. As well, aah well
Ah Lord. Long fingered are our sorrows.

& the afterlife three minutes eighteen seconds long,
& the afterlife is flying endlessly
& the distance & the blackness & the cold immense,

Ah well aahh well, ummm ummm.
Ah Lord Ah Lord Lord
Permit our afterlives to be so blessed.

Hey, Joe

DAVID WOJAHN

For Hendrix it's a sweet slow blues, Stratocaster
      pummeling leisurely the opening bars,
           a gracile firestorm that Mitchell's drums

and Redding's bass must fan and chisel, 4/4 stabs,
      the conflagration firewalling, as Jimi
           asks him where he's *going with that money*

in his hand, that *cold blue steel .44,*
      the questions almost querulous. The Leaves
           and the Byrds do it faster, lyrics slurred with shock,

and Willy de Ville implores it to strings,
      a Mariachi band, accordion-slathered to his
           lounge-lizard croon. But Hendrix knows

the song is gallows tree and killing floor,
      that death angels turn his wall incarnadine,
           definitive. The ceremonious blood.

He must take both parts—killer and chorus, strophe
      and antistrophe forged from feedback of an amp
           hiked up to ten. *Where you goin' with*

that blood . . . your hands. . . . I heard you shot
      your woman down. Fadeout and the jukebox lights
           have dimmed. And Bill shambles back toward

our table, balancing a foamy pitcher. The no-time
      of early afternoon, and Nick's is empty,
           the drinkers Dantescan, the barkeep channel surfing

until he crests on Court TV, pre-trial motions
            with the sound turned low, the nattering lawyers
                        resplendent with their clipboards and Armanis,

the aging football star expressionless, jotting notes
            while a rumpled coroner aims a magic marker
                        at a drawing of a face, of a woman's slit throat,

x's and arrows to mark trajectories.
            And even photos of the murdered woman's *dog*.
                        "They're saving the hi-tech stuff for later," says Bill,

and I answer that the pot we've smoked
            sneaks up on you. What Circle can this be, the gavel
                        flickering in the judge's fist, and Bill

rhapsodic over "Foxy Lady"'s chord progressions,
            then his segue to precognition, how Jung
                        dreamed World War I, *a monstrous flood, uncounted*

thousands drowned, the whole sea turned to blood . . . ? What Circle
            where the football player's puffy, once-cherubic face
                        gives way to med-lab footage, white coats

sloshing beakers, then the blurred-paisley twitch
            of cell division, fat DNA on all four TVs,
                        metaphase and anaphase, beside a team

of bar-light Clydesdales? What Circle? *Where you*
            goin' with that gun? . . . How comes it now
                        that thou art out of hell? Interphase,

prophase, and the whole sea foaming blood,
            pushing Mostar to page five, and bringing the dog
                        who must bark through it all, the knife weaving in,

who circles and barks, manic panting against
the shouts. The leaps, the choke chain loose
against the reddened slick cement,

falling back each time until his flank
is lathered and drenched, circle and wail, his slippery
paw prints to be mapped and measured, circles

in circles, tightening, his howl against ensanguined cries,
until it seems he turns to us, his muzzle
pulsing huge from every screen, the click

of his nails as he paws at the nether world's gates.

World Tree

DAVID WOJAHN

> *... it is considered best to choose a tree that has been*
> *struck by lightning.*
> —MIRCEA ELIADE, *SHAMANISM*

Format I: 78

——1957

Hank Williams is thick shellac. Hank Williams
is so lonesome he could cry. & in the basement my father stands,

the black grooves' slick pomade atremble in his hands.
Lonesome whippoorwill.
                        The saber saw hums

& stutters off. He needles the lonesome again.
Weary weary blues from waiting. This the procedure,

this the rite. At the doorway I hover
unseen, awl & woodscrew. My Zorro cape's an apron.

Tick, tick tick when the needle closes circle,
goodbye Joe.
                Copper glint of bourbon bottle

two-thirds gone, shoved back to where it's hidden on the shelf
behind the woodstain & the turpentine. Needle closes circle,

tick, tick. Bladewail, sawdust. Lost Highway,
take these chains.
                Startled, he turns to me.

Format II: 8-Track & Selectric

—1977

Startled, she turns from a reverie
two parts gin, one part *The Soundtrack to Dr. Zhivago,*

its recipe unvarying. Turns to me
as ice cubes rattle & the balalaikas swell.

My mother jams the squat red cartridge in the stereo—
violin murk over tape hiss,
      the tinny sleigh bells

conspiring to
     a confessional poem. My IBM Selectric
awaits like a phaeton, Courier 10-point

incising its mirrorball, elegant serifs
that are never my life,
      nor hers. A swig

or two more & she's out. The ice cubes
melt, for it's spring in the Urals.
      The sleigh is mudlocked

but the poem goes on, & the ball will rotate
to its melody of brittle grief, black acetate.

Format III: 45

—1964

"Don't Worry, Baby"'s falsetto of grief: the sleek black wax
coaxed from its sleeve, where the Beach Boys in identical stripes

are all grin & tan. But dread lurks
in the high notes & the bass line. The race

is tomorrow. The narrative is pure *High Noon*.
"I can't back down now . . . "
                                                    Panic in the voice

of Brian Wilson, who has "pushed the other guy too far." Soon
it all will change. The surfboard of innocence

will wipe out & drown. Dead cosmonauts will wheel in space.
The other guy
                        will lose both legs in Laos.

But now Brian's girl shall look him in the face,
commending him not to fear.
                                            The Jag gleams & purrs.

My mind's eye turns it Cinemascope, color resolution
Alamogordo bright.
                            I set the needle down again.

Format IV: Field Recordings

—1937

The drum is sinew, feather & reindeer skin,
fashioned from tree struck by lightning.

Static from a microphone, the cylinder is creaking.
Drumbeat. Argu Banyat moaning.
                              He ascends

The World Tree, eyes aflutter, a realm where Dr. Markov
cannot follow. The yurt is gray with smoke.

Rung by rung & branch by branch. The dead speak
birdsong, wolf-howl. Drumbeat.
                              He arrives

at their camp. They are phantom shape & animal soul,
adrift in the Other World's
                              boundless forests.

Drumbeat. 6,000 versts to the west,
gulag labor gouges out
                    the White Sea Canal.

Decrees are signed—the latest purge. Drumbeat,
birdsong, wolf-howl. The dead & their guttering speech.

Format V: 33 1/3

—1965

Alamogordo bright—I set the needle down again
on "Desolation Row." Postcards of the hanging

as the marchers pour across the Pettus Bridge—
then the clubs, the dogs unleashed,
                              the fire hoses seething

at the center of a low dishonest decade
where selves grow immense, then shrink

to pinpoint size, flickering like fireflies.
O the ghost of electricity
                    howls ectoplasmic

in the bones of all our faces. Dylan
stands frail with his Strat at Newport

Gotterdammerung loud on "Maggie's Farm."
Tear-gassed King retreats to Selma. Cronkite

in a flight suit narrates bombs above Hannoi.
Lord Self sets the bitter diamond down again.

Format VI: Cassette

—1994

Pearling from me, the sticky bitter salt.
Her tongue & my sudden groan. This

swallowed too, for we hadn't touched in months.
Pewter morning,
                the first snow of her last year hissing soft.

I am called upon to reconstruct the room,
though it was almost bare. Marianne Faithfull,

nicotine-ravaged, unspooling "Sister Morphine,"
"Strange Weather"
                from a battered boombox. I am called upon

to watch her rise & scurry to the dresser,
flipping the tape in the room's sudden chill

& all over the world—the precise guttural
moan—*strangers*
                talk only 'bout the weather.

I am called upon to summon up her face, her hand
against her mouth,
                & the tape & the snow circle on.

Format VII: CD

—2004

& thus the dead convene: the voices swirl on,
missives from the afterlife,
       laser-guided like a bomb,

chronicling this Exodus, this dreadlocked dream,
of endtime & deliverance. Marley's "Redemption

Song," given voice by the gravel majesty
of dead Johnny Cash,
       duetting with the dead

Joe Strummer, trading verses, shaky harmony
at the chorus, the unchained paradise of Garvey.

O won't you help me sing—Cash with his Lion
of Judah growl—
      these songs of freedom. Strummer

a beat behind, but lo the voices entwine.
The righteous shall prevail. The Downpresser

topple & break like a reed. The dead arisen.
Our offering: these plates of silver in our hands.

Format VIII: Download, Shamanic

Let go the dead, somber from their backdrops
        of extravagant azaleas. Let go
                their faces from the Spirit World,

sepia their corporal's stripes, black & white
        their scarved profiles, posing gravely,
                vamping for their jacket photos.

Let go the dead, return. Morning in summer,
        Noelle asleep at last, up half the night
                with our sons until the fevers broke.

Let go the dead. Upstairs the boys
        are waking, murmuring in their beds
                to one another from the dreams

of four-year-olds, cartoon balloon
        & sound collage, monsters sprouting
                multiple eyes, yet no more fearsome

than the shouted stammer
        of Joey Ramone, the *gabba gabba hey*
                the boys love to pogo to in their playroom.

Fast song again please, fast song again.
        Their feet stomp above me. Let go the dead,
                return. Invoke the spirit helpers

in the Secret Language, for the journey back
        is perilous. Summon the raven. Summon
                the owl. Drumbeat pulsing the Spirit World

where all speech arrives as song.
        Language remade. Language prolonged.
                The spirit helpers leave their perches.

By the skin drum they are summoned.
      Let go the dead, return
           through the pathways & the airwaves,

sing the rungs of the World Tree,
      song of three chords, song of abreaction.
           The dead are countenanced, let go.

The dead arisen. From the cul de sacs
      of neural mazes, return, from wax
           & acetate, from the white diamond light

lasering words to our ears, return.
      Verse chorus verse. 7 a.m.,
           the second of June. Above me

the boys dance circles until
      the ceiling trembles. *Gabba gabba*
           hey. Fast song again please.

Return, return. It is here that I
      shall dwell. The morning blazes up
           & my speech shall not be confounded.

Slide Guitar

KEVIN YOUNG

Tonight I wake with mud
in my head, a thick

brown I sink
my line into. Fists

full of fish.
Tonight even the storm

cannot calm me.

My hands tonight scatter
about the place, folded

quiet like a fine lady's gloves.
Cue the saddish music—

how like flies it rises!

Outside, the suicides
float by buoyant

in their lead balloons.

Blues

KEVIN YOUNG

Gimme some fruit
Gimme some fruit
Fresh salted melon
maybe some mango too

You had me eating pork ribs
You had me eatin ham
You had me so I was feedin
straight out your hand

Gimme some fruit, baby
Gimme some fru-uit
Something red
& juicy I can sink
these teeths into

You had me eating peas Lord
You had me eatin spam
(You had me so turned round)
I never dreamt all you said
came straight out a can

Gimme some fruit
Gimme some fru-uit
Gimme something strong girl
to clear my system of you

You served me up
like chicken
You deviled me like ham
Alls the while I never knew
you had another man

Gimme some fruit girl
Gimme some tomato too
What else is a poor
carnivore like me
without you supposed to do

Disaster Movie Theme Music

KEVIN YOUNG

Winding back roads
I believe in you

Winding muddy back roads
I say I believe in you

Wheels got stuck baby
What good's belief do?

—

Train in my way
Can't hardly cross

Train in the road babe
I couldn't hardly cross

By the time I got
to mom'n thems

Heard tell you
were a-ready lost

—

Cyclone hit and
tore my town apart

Cyclone hit town
Tore us clear apart

O how that swift
freight train sound

made off with my heart

—

Standing at your back door
The dogs bark so loud

Knocking on your back door
Till your dog barks so loud

As many times I come here girl
Now I'm not allowed?

—

Creek done risen
Creek done rose

It ain't the creek that
took off all them clothes

—

Lightning struck me once girl
Thunder sounded twice

Lightning struck me once now
Thunder hollered twice

Caught you in the kitchen, huh
Sipping cold red wine

—

Doctor told me wait son
Your heart it's beating faint

Doctor told me wait now
My thick heart beating faint

When I saw you kissing on him
You thought I'd be fit

and tied—I ain't.

—

So when it is you hear me
shutting your screen door

So when you hear me banging
shut your sweet screen door

Don't expect to see my
brown behind no more.

—

Walking toward the pickup
head inside my heart

Walking toward my Ford
echo inside my heart

Keep on turning clutch
and key

Won't hardly start

Yes, Yes, Y'all:

Poems about Hip-Hop

Hip Hop Analogies

TARA BETTS

after Miguel and Erykah Badu

If you be the needle
      I be the LP.
If you be the buffed wall,
      I be the Krylon.
If you be the backspin,
      I be the break.
If you be the head nod,
      I be the bass line.
If you be a Phillie,
      I be the razor.
If you be microphone,
      then I be palm.
If you be cipher,
      then I be beatbox.
If you be hands thrown up,
      then I be yes, yes, y'all.
If you be throwback,
      then I be remix.
If you be footwork,
      then I be uprock.
If you be turntable,
      then I be crossfader.
If you be downtown C train,
      then I be southbound Red Line.
If you be shell toes,
      then I be hoodie.
If you be freestyle,
      then I be piece book.
If you be Sharpie,
      then I be tag.

If you be boy,
      then I be girl
      who wants to
      sync samples
      into classic.

A Lesson from the Terrordome

Tara Betts

Echoes of sirens blared while phrases
belted from the boom of Chuck D's voice,
left imprints sinking into memory
that bob up when buoyant history
is necessary. The blast and thump
of "Welcome to the Terrordome" droned
intent with Flavor Flav's clock swinging
on his neck, a manic shining searchlight
beaming from a Black Planet that still
embodies fear and chaos for some.

When the dancers marched and pivoted
in lockstep military formation in front
of a target with crosshairs imposed
on a black man's silhouette, Chuck D
insisted to everyone in earshot come
on down. The sample's rapid response
get down fired back, but the internal
rhyme in "the shooting of Huey Newton"
never left my head. It sent me, curious,
to a small, Midwestern library, before
internet searches streamed into houses.

So, my finger traced columns
in an antiquated guide to periodicals, flipped
through a card catalog's long shelves,
looked for N's, then Newton. Who was he?

When I clicked the microfiche onto spindle
and rolled through articles moving cross
a white screen, squares of photos and text

rolled one frame at a time until the brief
article appeared—*Black Panther Found Dead
in Oakland*. I shook my head and silently
asked how much of the story is missing,
how I wouldn't even know about the bullet
dropping Newton, if Chuck hadn't told me.

"Runaway" Premiers in Los Angeles on October 18, 2010

SARAH BLAKE

MTV.com reported: At the end of his speech, West touched briefly on his mother's death and how he isn't scared of anything because he feels as though everything has been taken away from him. "I have no mother, no grandmothers, no girlfriend, no daughter, and I lived with a woman my whole life," he said.

Kanye is 33. If he were Jesus, he would die this year,
and be resurrected.

> *I can't unthink this thought.*

He said he had considered suicide, but found his life to be that
   of a soldier's,
"a soldier for culture."

> *Some men are kept alive by fighting.*

> *I don't want this for you, Kanye.*

To the right of the article is a video clip of an interview.

> " . . . both me and George express ourselves with our truest,
>   our truest vision . . . "

Kanye's bottom teeth distract me.
If I ever questioned whether the diamonds were there,
they're there.

> *You're all kinds of beautiful.*

And if that's not a word I can use, you're
resplendent, numinous, healthy.

I am two months pregnant.

Monday this premiere, Tuesday this article, Wednesday
my first ultrasound, with my child's boneless arms in motion.

A memory I didn't know I could have.

Thursday I write—If I have a daughter, you can hold her.
  A son, too.

The two of you, tied to this week in my life.

Ha Ha Hum

SARAH BLAKE

In the chorus of one of my favorite songs are three throat-clearing
    sounds—
sometimes depicted as *Ha Ha Hum*
on lyrics websites such as azlyrics.com, lyricstime.com, and
    anysonglyrics.com

A sound we make when we talk with the mouths of Jews.
        Channukah, l'chaim, chutzpah.
Voiceless fricative.

Russians have a letter for it. In block, an *x*, in Cyrillic, two *c*'s back
    to back.
In the words, good, *chorrosho*, and bad, *plocho*.
They have other letters I love, for *sh, tss, sht, szh, yoo.*

The sound Kanye makes—it's not unlike the French *r*.
How my name falls back into the mouth like it's collapsing.
        Sa-cha.

In Russian, the *r* would roll, as when my great-grandmother said
    her name,
as when my great-grandfather called to her.
My name means *princess* in Hebrew.

Kanye's means *the only one* in Swahili.
A language once written in Arabic script, now written with letters
    like ours.
Switched in the 1800's. Trying for sounds like *nz* and *nd*, to begin
    words.

The mouths we speak with are hidden by our other mouths.

Like the Poems Do

SARAH BLAKE

I ask,
    "Who's that?"
and Noah answers,
    "Mos Def."

    "Is Kanye rapping like Snoop Dogg there?"
    "No. His jaw is wired shut,"

Another song,
    "Is that Common?"
    "Yes. They're friends. They're both from Chicago."

Noah's been listening
to rap since middle school. He used to make tapes
off the radio and listen to them until they broke.

I grew up saying, I listen to everything but country
and rap.

Recently, I spent another evening researching Kanye.
This time
about his 2004 debut album, *College Dropout.*

"Through the Wire" came out fast, without permission for the
    sample of Chaka Khan's "Through the Fire."

I tell Noah. We're on our computers,
across the room.
He pulls up Khan's song; I pull up Kanye's music video.

The room is a mess of sound.

I tell Noah how Kanye kisses his hand, places it
on a larger-than-life poster of Khan.

Is there a poem of Kanye as a teenager, loving
the woman who sings, too,
"I'm Every Woman"?

A smaller poster in his smaller room.

Noah with posters of Erykah Badu and Lauryn Hill,
if he were the sort of boy to have posters.

Noah and I move to the bedroom soon,
and every night. Noah lets me
                            bring Kanye in,
knows our life has room for all of it.

The Message

MICHAEL CIRELLI

Malcolm was fed 16 bullets because of his. A slug kissed
the jaw of King Jr. and silenced him forever. Gandhi shriveled
like snakeskin. Joan of Arc became Joan of Ash—
So you can understand why Melle Mel was jittery scribbling it
all down, on a napkin, at Lucky's Noodle Shop in Harlem.
Sweat pearled into his green tea. He thought of Jesus
hanging from that dull wood. Heard about the poet Lorca
under an olive tree, shot in the back. Everyone has felt this way though,
he thought. Never could he imagine what would happen
when he pressed his thumbprint into vinyl. Hip-hop was still
a tadpole. The DJ had just learned to scratch a record and make sounds
no ear had ever conjugated. How was he to know Tupac & Biggie
would follow his lead and get plugged with lead? So he wrote it down,
in big curling letters, emphatic: *don't push me.*

Love Song for Kelis

Michael Cirelli

I can't compare your voice
to Sarah Vaughn's

sassy tabernacle,
or to Ella's frantic sidestep

up a fire escape on a sticky
night in Chocolate City,

not even to the impenetrable
vaults in Holiday's lungs,

or Nina Simone's sad
peach, with a crew cut.

Your voice is not hash smoke
swirling around an antique fan

in Amsterdam, or the strong finger
of bourbon on my chest,

or Tina Turner's electric
hairdo. It may be simply

the best baby, but it is still
nothing like Chaka Khan's

bottom lip after lovemaking—
I can see how some might think

that your voice is the milky
cherry drowning at the bottom

of a Harlem shake, or that
holding your CD next to my face

in the mirror is the picture
of a perfect couple. And I know

your husband's father is a mediocre jazz great,
but my dad is a cook, ringing bells

when eggs are hot. (I will use
this against you if ever I get a chance.)

I know your voice is sugar
honey iced tea with a striped straw,

and though I may never get a sip, even so,
it still makes my body go *yeah yeah.*

Lobster with Ol' Dirty Bastard

MICHAEL CIRELLI

The broken-down fishing boats on the dock rock back and forth
as if there is music in the air. Norma Jean, Captain's Girl, Jenny, all
    hips and
bounce—*shimmy shimmy ya* in their slips. Across the street,
    Randazzo's Clam Bar,
"the pride of Sheepshead Bay," bustles. Inside, not a fisherman nor
    pirate, but rapper
Ol' Dirty Bastard has his own seat, where he reigns with sunglasses
    and a vinyl bib.
Dirty *likes it raw,* so raw he fathered 13 children, and when he rolls
    up to Randazzo's,
in his black school bus with 24-inch rims, his clan of offspring
    pour out like bass.
Mama Randazzo sighs and smiles that forced diagonal smile, as
    she drags 6 tables together.
There are platters of mussels and little necks with mouths wide
    open!
Dinner rolls bounce off the walls like handballs! Sword fights
    break out with shrimp
skewers, the toddlers wear calamari rings on their fingers like
    diamonds, and lil' Rusty
does the fake-sneeze-trick that leaves an oyster in his open palm.
    Ol' Dirty is ravishing
a huge boiled lobster, drawn butter dripping down his chin, as he
    cracks open the claws
with his golden fangs.

KRS-1 Sleeps at Prospect Park

MICHAEL CIRELLI

On cold nights, the blue lips of Lord Krishna
would whisper Ralph Waldo Emerson to sleep, and in
Emerson's dreams, words would build a home at the edge
of a deep lake. The fir trees called the names of all the ghosts
of England, and Krishna blew a dagger out the side of a conch—
Many years later, on the Eastern Parkway side of Prospect Park,
where drummers meet on Sundays to subpoena their homelands,
a young KRS-1 eats a Jamaican patty under an elderberry bush.
He writes *Black Cop* on the wax paper. He lies on the ground
where the Battle of Long Island was fought against British soldiers
who never questioned their government. The stars in the sky
are ghosts that he knows are there, and he dreams of the South Bronx
that spit him out like a watermelon seed. Under his head rests
Self-Reliance like a pillow.

When Talib Kweli Gets Expelled from Brooklyn Tech

MICHAEL CIRELLI

He doesn't slam Principal Grabowski's door like a gavel.
He doesn't put on his Yankees hat, in defiance. No middle finger
to the security guard or loogie on the glossy tile. He walks,
his head not high nor slouched, down the corridor and not one
student points or cackles like a hyena. Jon Taylor inserts text
into his ear, beneath the pitch of the bell—as they exchange
ancient Kemetic handshakes—and move on.
Under Ms. Browne's door, he slips his book report like an oil spill.
He shakes the physics teacher's hand firm as apples. He winks
a rainbow at secretary Ignatius Butler, and opens those heavy blue
    doors
one last time. It is fall. Winter is showing its baby teeth and the sun
is carrying two hundred spindles of saffron to Florida. The leaves
are like cinder footprints leading to Ft. Green Park. He sits beneath
an oak tree, pulls the book from his backpack, and starts reading
    again, *Beloved*.

Phife Dawg Awaits a Kidney

Michael Cirelli

and his mother is patient as an olive tree. She understands
the thick accent of dialysis, isn't fooled by the organ's rhetoric.
Instead, she marvels at the fluid that scrubs her son's blood
    clean—
makes metaphors about this science-water. She is a poet too, first.
When he was a child she'd belt out Braithwaite verses, as she
    slipped
insulin into his reluctant arm. Now, she watches as the catheter is
    prepared
for the funky diabetic, who is thirsty. It enters like his first kiss,
    from Janet Wilkinson,
under a black moon, on Linden Boulevard, represent represent.
    Chemistry moves
in his stomach like venom. For a moment he feels like he is going
    to die.
He wishes some god would roll up in a white Escalade, stick his
    fist out the window
to drop a shiny new kidney in his palm, as a husky voice booms,
    It's all good Diggy.
His mother sits beside him on the bed, studying each name on her
    list meticulously.
She is walking along every branch of their family tree—further
    and further out
onto each limb, trying to find a match in the leaves.

the cash register in Dr. Dre's head goes bling

I thought he would be able to get away
with saying a lot more than I would . . .
                              —DR. DRE

KEVIN COVAL

jimmy iovine pressed play in his beverly hills garage

                              and the tornado sirens moaned
in the trees, lightbulbs exploded into handclap casio synths
fuck you pay me mantras, twisting knobs in front of the soundboard.

Dre flew the kid on the tape from Detroit to LA two days later.

this is the fox of history smiling in the chicken coop
the Nile rushing north, cows butchering the butcher
wade in the water on *YO! mtv raps*, opposite day, the faint
hum of reparations massaged out worn hands in the field. it struck
him clear as lightning. he is no ben franklin, but this is just
what the doctor ordered.

robert van winkle has some tough decisions to make

KEVIN COVAL

there were two deals on the table.

Chuck D wanted to sign him[1]
have the Bombsquad work
production. if there was gonna be
a rap L-vis, he'd like to get paid
to have a hand in the molding
this time.

and there was capitol records
and their million dollar signing bonus.
and Robert's foreign two-seat junker
at the mechanic. he'd never seen
that much negative space before
in the bellies of all those zeroes

the mouths of six ghosts
macaulay culkin, frozen, alone.

[1] (i know, i couldn't believe that shit either)

the beastie boys cast a video for paul's boutique

Kevin Coval

cabernet bottles, ounces of herb, mounds of cash
line the conference table, three upper east side boys

wear afro-wigs, inebriated grins. a fledgling punk
band turned hip-hop by the downtown eighties and Fab 5 Freddie.

signed to capitol records, grown men, money to burn, casting
the *hey ladies* video at a los angeles hotel. coddled by television

they loved Rudy Ray Moore's bug eyes, watermelon, chicken bones
mercedes hood ornaments above their crib. silver blunts in their
    mouths.

near the Pacific today, a line of bikinis around a door, down the
    hall, flesh
paraded at auction for the boys who are beastly. for the boys
    behind

a conference table in afro-wigs. whiteboys in afros' wigs. they are
    not Black.
the joke is they are not Black.

The Crossover

Kevin Coval

it was the end of disco. all the jobs were moving or changing or drying up in the city like the river after a summer of no rain. the parents moved farther from the city or themselves or their families for those jobs. hours in commute. we received a key to let ourselves in after school. they would not be home till late. sometimes they would not be home at all. sometimes the commute was too much. the parents too far gone to see each other. busy running around. sometimes running around with other parents. sometimes running around doing things parents shouldn't do.

there were plenty of tvs and radios. there were older siblings. city/suburban sleepover camps. there was a black friend. a new york cousin. a late night pbs airing of henry chalfant's documentary. there was a leak. it was run dmc. it was newcleus's *jam on it.*

the house was quiet. peanut butter spread on crackers. sandwiched potato chips. there was bruce lee, saturday afternoon shoguns. kamala the ugandan giant. nothing was explained. no one home to contextualize. everything was mixed up. ninjas wore black like ice cube. burn hollywood. the sleeper hold. the college radio political talk show said south africa.

there was apartheid at the schools. apartheid in the lessons we sat thru. nelson mandela was in america. his name was chuck d. his name was krs-one. what is a Black Panther? there is apartheid on the bus home. there is apartheid in the lunchroom. the sides of the city we don't visit. were told not to. there is apartheid on the television. bill cosby aside.

there was a tape deck. a walkman. there was no apartheid in the music. no separation in the library. books endlessly check-out-able. there was holden. the hero Huey P. the wandering protagonist in the midst of all that quiet. the new music to soundtrack the walk to school. the music truthed. the music was middle finger fuck you. fuck you actor reagan who sent uncle dave crazy back into the streets. fuck you actor reagan who warred on the drugs my mom did. what you know about three jobs and two kids and running from landlords. the music was solace and ammunition. alone and one in the chamber.

i listened to every word. memorized all the words. recited the words into a notebook. there was not a viaduct in the music. there was not a neighborhood to avoid. there was not a gunnery filled with columbus broken promises. there was not a cold war of white flight and divorced unions. there was a hero. for the people. all of the people.

i wanted to be a hero.

molemen beat tapes

KEVIN COVAL

were copped from Gramophone.
cassettes jammed into a factory
issued stereo deck of the hoopty
i rolled around in. a bucket. bass
and drum looped with some string
sample, fixed. a sliver of perfect
adjusted. the scrapes of something
reconstituted. there was so much
space to fill. an invitation to utter.
Iqra—Allah said to the prophet
Muhammad (peace be upon Him).
a- to b-side and around again. a circle
a cipher. i'd drive down and back
in my mom's dodge for the latest
volumes of sound. i'd stutter
and stop and begin again. lonesome
and on fire. none. no one i knew
rapped. i'd recite alone on Clark St.
free, styling, shaping, my voice
a sapling, hatchling, rapping
my life, emerging in the dark
of an empty car.

·

there was a time when hip-hop felt like a secret
society of wizards and wordsmiths. magicians
meant to find you or that you were meant to find
like rappers i listened to and memorized in history
class talked specifically me, for me.

·

& sometimes
you'd see a kid whisper to himself
in the corner of a bus seat & you
asked if he rhymed & traded a poem
a verse like a fur pelt/trapping.
some gold or food. this sustenance.

you didn't have to ride solo anymore.

•

Jonathan was the first kid i met who rapped. he was Black
from a prep school, wore ski goggles on top his head & listened
to Wu-Tang which meant he was always rhyming about science
and chess. his pops made him read Sun-Tzu. his mans was Omega
a fat Puerto Rican who wrote graffiti and smoked bidis.

& they'd have friends
& the back seat would swell
& the word got passed/scooped like a ball
on the playground. you'd juggle however long
your mind could double dutch. sometimes you'd take
what you were given/lift off like a trampoline
rocket launch. sometimes you'd trip & scrape
your knees. tongue-tied, not quick. words stuck
on loop, like like words, stuck, like that. but break
thru, mind, knife sharp, mind darts
polished & gleaming we'd ride
for the sake of rhyming. take the long way
home or wherever the fuck we were going
cruise down Lake Shore & back, blasting
blazing. polishing these gems.
trying to get our mind right.

Fight the Power (Public Enemy, 1989)

STEPHEN CRAMER

The lyrics showcase Chuck D's politics,
          but the video mostly displays Flav's
lunatic persona: his crazy-eyed antics
          as he flashes a gold-toothed grin—*Yeah boyee!*—& raves

while the clock looped around his neck flows
          with his sway & counter-sway. The song's about
revolt, about how most of their heroes
          don't appear on no stamps. But however they shout

& politic, all people across the nation
          want to know is *what's up with the clock?*
Chuck D don't care. (Go ahead, let them obsess.) Chuck
          D knows that the train's pulling into the station,

because this is the end of the line.
He knows the clock & song both say: it's about *time.*

Rising Down (The Roots, 2008)

STEPHEN CRAMER

It's not what you'd expect to hear when you go
       to the mall, but there it is: the repeated
chime to shake us out of our slumber: *hello*
       hello hello hello. The rhythm creeps

along, the opposite of the shoppers rushing
       from store to store, balancing ziggurats
       of boxes in this season of want. Yeah, so what,
it's 80 degrees in Alaska? Just airbrush

       the ice back in. You still need to get your
       Super Laser Blaster Retaliator.
So go ahead & pay, then hold out
your hands to receive the future you've bought.

& no offense, sir, I don't mean to be drastic,
but *how you want it bagged, paper or plastic?*

O.P.P.

KYLE DARGAN

It was Magic that summer. Our tracks were long
—spooled between the hubs of Crescent Road
and Prospect Street. Sound we carried on foot
from one avenue to the other. Apartment buildings'
walls and sunken garages kept us from cutting
through back yards, kept us moving in knights' Ls—
intersection to intersection, long boulevards
made for rooks or teenagers whose urban costumes
fit them ill as legacies.

                        Climbing to the top floor
in one of Prospect's proud brick towers, already
were Mrs. Roach and my grandmother cooking
words. Speculation stewed between them. I watched
lips pause for news. California | Earvin Johnson | HIV.
Around me, they spat "tsk" and guessed at Cookie's fate.

Down Park, over Glenwood to Jason's driveway court.
A game of 21—running hookshots tolled his backboard
while all we asked was "You heard?" We understood
little of what made "the hiv" and swore by our own
foolishness that we knew how to prevent it.
In Jason's bedroom studio we freestyled goofy lyrics,
deepened our voices to castigate. "Should've
used a prophylactic" I barked like a Cypress Hill
chorus or a Kane crescendo: put a quarter in your ass
'cause you just played yourself. Years later I would
be shamed—the health teacher correcting me
on the role mouths can play in transmission.

Terror was knowing I was one wrong answer away
from being like Magic. Maybe one pair of lips
—another's, my own. I want to go back and rescind
those lips that made rhymes as a child. Remember,
we'd just sealed the '80s. Reagan's vacant smile
haunted our homes, hip-hop was too busy
for compassion, and we fashioned ourselves fly
as we wove music of other people's pain.

Turning the Tables

JOEL DIAS-PORTER

for Eardrum

First hold the needle
   like a lover's hand
Lower it slowly
   let it tongue
   the record's ear
Then cultivate
the sweet beats
   blooming in the valley
   of the groove
Laugh at folks
   that make requests
What chef would let
   the diners determine
Which entrees
   make up the menu?
Young boys
   think it's about
flashy flicks
   of the wrist
But it's about filling the floor
   with the manic
   language of dance
About knowing the beat
of every record
   like a mama knows
   her child's cries
Nobody cares
how fast you scratch

Cuz it ain't about
    soothing any itch
It's about how many hairstyles
    are still standing
At the end of the night.

Preface to a 20 Volume Homicide Note

after Amiri Baraka

KRISTA FRANKLIN

Today I turned *Transbluesency* over
to the hands of a teenager tussling
with her own words, still trying to decipher
the difference between invention and insipidness.
Meanwhile, you know, the world whips against
our hunched shoulders and McKay's call to arms
is buried in the graveyards of the poets' imaginings,
its ghost inhabiting some young soul in Egypt,
rumbling in the heart of Libya. Meanwhile,
America picks the lint from its navel, moonwalks
its way back to antebellum inertia, lulls itself
to sleep with airwave regurgitations of 1970
before music sold its soul for a stripper pole.

At your lecture, we sat in the Amen Corner
and *hallelujahed* your every word, knowing
over half that room didn't know Tyner from
Tyson, couldn't pick Monk out from a mugshot.
Meanwhile, while knee-grows still swallowing
the jizz of the American Dream and south-
side Chicago teens juke Africa in hyper-speed,
we still ain't caught up where we need to be,
more concerned with how much gold we can
dig out a broke nigga's pocket, debating the political
incorrectness of the word *bitch*, and which came
first: the pimp smack or the egging. Baldwin broke
himself writing tomes on black love while chain
smoking and dragging racism out to the streets
by the scruff of its dirty neck, all to be reduced
to "the gay dude?" in the college classroom.

Who's gonna save us now that all the black heroes
are running from the cops holding their pants
up with dusty fingers they never deigned
to open a book with? Black heroes more concerned
with erasing their records and record deals
than delving into solving the algebra of black agony,
bolt-cutting the inextricable chains of imperialism
that got everybody tied up in knots. Who's gonna
save us now that all the black heroes are making
it rain in sweatshops where the heroines calculate
payouts in booty-bounce, and the drum got
pawn-shopped for a machine?

Bottom Feeders

YOLANDA FRANKLIN

I wore unemployment like a shawl in Florida humidity the day FEMA was an off-duty lifeguard when Katrina lap danced over Nola, received an eviction notice in a section-8 community called Wellington, and survived a car crash in a Geo Prism that left me without the use of my hands for six weeks. The property developers of my apartment complex must have strategically chosen that symbolic meaning of the community name. They must have anticipated the necessity for the tenants of the community to wear *knee-length water-proof, rubber or plastic boots* in order to "pull yourselves up by your own bootstraps," even if you are a Black, educated, single-parent of two teenagers, who's been nominated for a Disney® Teaching Award. First thing every morning, in the 3/2 house I rented from a progressive-six-karats-in-total-daily-wear-Barbie, I brewed Café du Monde and watched Kanye from the couch say what every American Black was thinking and feeling while I hauntingly searched for my cousin, a chef on Bourbon Street, and my friend Nelson: "President Bush doesn't care about Black people!" It's been three months. I'm still waiting to get the foodstamps. Maybe he just cares about bootstraps. Maybe his colorblindness prevented him from seeing people sunbathing on the rooftops of the houses that were treading water like buoys. Maybe he thought that as long as Black people in the Bayou wear Wellingtons, they won't drown! Maybe he mistook them for a catfish or crawfish—any native bottom feeders of the sea.

Break

ARACELIS GIRMAY

When the boys are carnivals
we gather round them in the dark room
& they make their noise while drums
ricochet against their bodies & thin air
below the white ceiling hung up like a moon
& it is California, the desert. I am driving in a car,
clapping my hands for the beautiful windmills,
one of whom is my brother, spinning,
on a hillside in the garage
with other boys he'll grow old with, throw back.
How they throw back their bodies
on the cardboard floor, then spring-to, flying
like the heads of hammers hitting strings
inside of a piano.
                        Again, again.
This is how they fall & get back up. One
who was thrown out by his father. One
who carries death with him like a balloon
tied to his wrist. One whose heart will break.
One whose grandmother will forget his name.
One whose eye will close. One who stood
beside his mother's body in a green hospital. One.
Kick up against the air to touch the earth.
See him fall, then get back up.
Then get back up.

These Are the Breaks

Idris Goodwin

You've heard the myths and legends. '70s south Bronx. Poly-culture pot of gold, echo urban stomps. Hands releasing ratchets to touch the vinyl, stroke the grooves. Nodding back and forth like wrists that found new ways to prove. And show, and grow, and blend. Bring it back again. Edit. Gut. And tear new names up out the wind.

You've heard about criminal. The daring, death-defying, so-called underground. So-called urban styling. With the Asian technology that flooded the colony. Bytes of info, bit and flip.

Tools inverted. Sound stolen and distorted like legislation imported. Stolen like real estate, inventions and credit. Broken like neighborhoods when interstates arrive.

So the children of the losing war, they built a bridge again. Pulse to pulse catapults, lasso pulling different folks on subway cars, on foot or spokes called Philosophical. Diasporic.

The magical mining through mud for the fantastical. Celebrating. Chanting out: Raw, strike, flame ignite. Heart, livid, never break for the night.

For blocks and blocks, hips-head. Let the Breakers break. The stale left dead.

Yes,
we ex
plode
on the
break is the place where the poem get laced. Let the rhythm hit us first in the face.

And,
in bet
ween,
all these
bangs and the bumps and the pows and the thumps, we explore time's
signature, we can't get enough.

And,
to this
day,
the words we
say been influenced by the molding of music, changing it around for
a brand new usage.

New Bird riding horse with Bach. So-called third world pulled into
the concerto. Some wanna cap, regulate madness. Scared of the
beautiful miscegenated scratches. But they never die down, they only
get live-er. Can't nobody copyright fire. Can't nobody copyright fire.
Can't nobody copyright fire.

'Cause it's spreadin' like it always do. Suburban, urban, and the rural,
too. Plugged in. Tucked in.

Finding new ways to tune in. Finding new ways to stand up. Speak
out. Get by. Finding new ways to say how long you been here.
Finding new ways to stop the erasure of markings.

Breaking down all the talking, coded, loaded, locked and smoking,
stocked. Because it be about the *body*, the body's reaction. The
lungs, throat, tongue. The limbs' rebellion.

Finding new ways to break the rhythm expected. Finding new ways
to break the laws of stolen land.

And some, they like to say they got patents on the noise. Numbers
on the invisible, barcodes on light. But fire, you can't copy, right?

Hip Hop on Adams Road

IDRIS GOODWIN

Van Hoosen Middle School was about a mile from my home and I'd walk. Sometimes my friend Jason would walk with me. Walking. Talking. Turned to popping turned to spitting. Then the spits went round and round, lips exploding. His whole body jumped.

Jason had discovered beat boxing. Sloppily, but he'd deciphered the code.

When Jason and I first met, he was Megadeth, Iron Maiden, Guns N Roses. I was Run Dmc, the Fat Boys, LL Cool J, Eazy E. Now here was Jason playing air drums with his mouth, motioning for me to join in.

"Make up your own rhymes," he said, and so I gave it a shot. Elementary at first, Dr. Seuss style. Hat, fat, cat. Two pre-teen boys throwing arms into high motion, a concert of spit and rhyme up Adams Road. Jason's face a bright red as confused cars inched by.

In the weeks that followed, Jason broke out his Yamaha electronic drum pad in attempt to duplicate his body's music, the kind that erupted from his mouth. But it wasn't the same. The beats he tapped with sticks lacked the round warmth of lungs, the authenticity of breath and skin. Next, we tried my Casiotone keyboard. The built-in microphone allowed for a few seconds of voice recording. We jammed the sun to sleep.

Day after day, we meandered through textbooks. Ate canned fish and defrosted green beans. Watched sitcoms. All the while, we thought about tomorrow's walk, and the day after that. Unable to sleep, brains beating out the rhythm of possibility.

Ode to Lil' Kim in Florence

Barbara Hamby

We're in a taxi on the way to see Andrea del Sarto's last supper,
      which was in the country when it was painted
but is now in the suburbs beyond the old city wall in an ex-convent,
      and our driver turns the radio to an English station
playing an American song, yes, Lil' Kim's "How Many Licks,"
      and Miss Kim, you are not singing about throwing punches,
but for a while I don't notice because my husband
      is talking about where we will eat dinner, but like a bullet
the lyrics penetrate the armor of the city, the fresco, the tagliata
      and puntarelle I'll eat later, and I'm crossing my legs twice,
once at the knees and then at the ankles, but what do I know,
      because my dad never threw me out of the house,
and I've never lived on the streets, and your life, Kim, is like an opera,
      Lucia di Lammermoor maybe, but you're not taking Enrico's shit,
and when Edgardo breaks into your phony wedding you grab him
      and run off to Paris but not before you sing the mad scene,
because what's *Lucia* without it, all the blood and tattoos, and you
      could never sing Mimi, because she's such a simp. No, Musetta's
your gal, so Lil' Kim put on your Queen-of-the-Night gown,
      the corset and headpiece with shooting stars, or your Lulu rags,
Jack the Ripper leading her to his knife, or your Lil' Kim hot pants,
      but remember, Kim, we girls need some secrets while we fix
our lipstick, straighten our push-up bras and little black dresses,
      because we're riding the lonely streets in taxis, limos,
buses and sports cars, hair a little messy, dying for the night to open up
      dark and mysterious like a song only time can sing.

When I Put My Hands in the Air It's Praise

Alysia Nicole Harris

In a club in Prague
      I'm wearing python-skin shoes,
tiger-print dress. All the Cosmic Dancer's foes

wrapped around my waist.
      Let the DJ be Shiva
spinning, with his four arms,

Bajan Rihanna atop Dre in South Central
      moves her body like a limpid snake—
            Let me show you how sacred hips can be.

A man prettier than crystal
      grinds his pelvis
into the small of my back.

I dance in his arms, and outside
      the snow isn't sharp,
there's just enough song left

to squeeze through. I lick the lyrics
      from inside his mouth
            What's the Czech word for *tonight?*

How do you say *the music*
      ain't Christian but swear-to-God
it's holy?

What It Look Like

Terrance Hayes

Dear Ol' Dirty Bastard: I too like it raw,
I don't especially care for Duke Ellington
at a birthday party. I care less and less
about the shapes of shapes because forms
change and nothing is more durable than feeling.
My uncle used the money I gave him
to buy a few vials of what looked like candy
after the party where my grandma sang
in an outfit that was obviously made
for a West African king. My motto is
Never mistake what it is for what it looks like.
My generosity, for example, is mostly a form
of vanity. A bandanna is a useful handkerchief,
but a handkerchief is a useless-ass bandanna.
This only looks like a footnote in my report
concerning the party. *Trill* stands for what is
truly real though it may be hidden by the houses
just over the hills between us, by the hands
on the bars between us. That picture
of my grandmother with my uncle
when he was a baby is not trill. What it is
is the feeling felt seeing garbagemen drift
along the predawn avenues, a sloppy slow rain
taking its time to the coast. Milquetoast
is not trill, nor is bouillabaisse. *Bakku-shan*
is Japanese for a woman who is beautiful
only when viewed from behind. Like I was saying,
my motto is *Never mistake what it looks like*
for what it is else you end up like that Negro

Othello. (Was Othello a Negro?) Don't you lie
about who you are sometimes and then realize
the lie is true? You are blind to your power, Brother
Bastard, like the king who wanders his kingdom
searching for the king. And that's okay.
No one will tell you you are the king.
No one really wants a king anyway.

emcee

TERRANCE HAYES

You get to wear triple X
Jeans for easy access to lair of first breaths

You get to reveal your shank
Handmade with a tooth of a bed spring and gauze

You get to rhyme about death—

Explicit lyrics, you are the pied piper
Sending children into jerk patterns and grunts
Into tunnels of smoke—

I had to get high to write this—

Your mind twists,
Gleams like lights on the bends of a night-coaster
The riders throw their hands in the air—

You get Grandmaster mantras—
And wave 'em like they just don't care

Under your spell I can do anything

Fly girls and Hoochie Mommas, La Femme Fantabulous
Writing your phone number on their tongues

Sucka emcees can call me Sire

Indelible tattoos
The night cut on like an open sentence—
You are the Alpha and the Omegaphone

The night cut and you won't ever be alone—
Your grin of gold-plated windows

You want the exit code from the tenement, the penitentiary—
You want [beatbox   beatbox   beatbox]

Breathlessness

Elegy, Fort Greene

"It was all a dream." —The Notorious B.I.G.

Anna Claire Hodge

North of me, you too are within walls
and won't prepare for the storm
that will move from here and hang
above your brownstone like
a cold mobile. Unlike me, you don't
stand in line for beer & bread
like tired parents in the grocery,
who on their hips balance children
swallowed by parkas like Lil' Kim
in her black mink who wailed watching
Biggie's funeral procession. She reached
out desperately toward the limousines
crowned by wreaths that snaked down
your street in Bedford-Stuyvesant
more than a decade ago. When you
pass your window, do you glance
down, & for a moment, think of the
neighborhood boys holding dollar bills
over candles purchased from the bodega
as the over-sized coffin passed in its hearse?
Their tribute to his childhood boasting:
one day he'd be rich enough to burn
money. The dollars, then the boys
turn to smoke. It was, in fact, all
a dream. So you return to your books,
count them in case of a wind that might lift
& steal a prized copy, read again a chapter
that always made you weep, or open

a can of beans and forget them on the counter
for a game of online chess. Probabilities
swirl above you like hallucinations, like
the spectacle of neon, my first night
in Atlantic City. In that suit at the Tropicana
you were really something, & taught me
just what to do. Always double down
& triple stack. Play the dozens. Tip
the dealer. Order Long Islands to get
your money's worth, but keep them
off the felt. If you win a black chip, call it
a night. Never forget to bet on zero,
because when you forget is when it hits.

Small Poems for Big

twenty-four haiku for each year he lived

CHINAKA HODGE

when you die, i'm told
they only use given names
christopher wallace

no notorious
neither b.i.g. nor smalls
just voletta's son

brooklyn resident
hustler for loose change, loosies
and a lil loose kim

let me tell you this
the west coast didn't get you
illest flow or nah

had our loyalties
no need to discuss that now
that your weight is dust

that your tongue is air
and your mother is coping
as only she can

i will also say
that i have seen bed-stuy since
b.k. misses you

her walk has changed some
the rest of the borough flails
weak about itself

middle school students
not yet whispers in nine sev
know the lyrics rote

you: a manual
a mural, pressed rock, icon,
fightin word or curse

course of history
most often noted, quoted
deconstructed sung

hung by a bullet
prepped to die: *gunsmoke gunsmoke*
one hell of a hunch

here you lie a boy
twelve-gauge to your brain you can't
have what you want be

what you want you black
and ugly heartthrob ever
conflicted emcee

respected lately
premier king of the casket
pauper of first life

til puff blew you up
gave you a champagne diet
plus cheese eggs, welch's

you laid the blueprint
gave us word for word for naught
can't fault the hustle

knockoff messiah
slanged cracked commandments, saw no
honey, more problems

a still black borough
recoiled, mourned true genius slain
the ease of your laugh

the cut of your jib
unique command of the room
truthfully biggie

what about you's small
no not legend not stature
real talk just lifespan

yo, who shot ya kid
n.y.p.d. stopped searching
shrugged off negro death

well, we scour the sky
we mourn tough, recite harder
chant you live again

of all the lyrics
the realest premonition
rings true: you're dead. wrong

2pac couplets

one line for each year he lived

CHINAKA HODGE

ninety six minutes after tyson wins and you're gone
las vegas quickly strips you of your last song

every black man in nevada pilgrims to trudge you
walk last rites, as only god can judge you

nomad, you baltimore, you new york, you l.a.
captured only by wind, a consummate stray

west coast makes you ours. claims you loudest
you gave game for free, we recoup it proudest

don't want no producers dancing in our videos
named our first born after brenda's embryo

your dear mama, eschews her crackfiend fame
afeni becomes household, recognized name

the people used to clown when you came around
with the underground mimic and savior your sound

mark your ink, the lives of thugs on their stomachs
their bottoms, their rolling twenties, their hunneds

your words so sacrament so memorized so litmus
test and testament so wretched so generous

never knew malcolm as machiavellian text, hence
you vexed and cursing: our black and shining prince

our sweetest thing, our prism and its light
lynched by a bullet, won't survive the knight

now your blood spills and the people crowd around
just one question:

                                                    r u
                                                    still
                                                    down?

Silk City

MAJOR JACKSON

No space
at the bar
so you stare
at the neon

signs blinking
in the mirror
behind the bottles.
Tiny flecks

of a stuccoed
ceiling glitter.
At a cocktail
table, colors flare

from a lava lamp,
illuminating
a couple bent
towards each other

like angels stilled
on a kiss. The disco
ball whirls, spinning
slow beams of light

from a million
lighthouses. You've
paid to enter so much
darkness. A shore

of human flesh
mingles. A crew
of cool cats lean
against glass

bricked windows,
bobbing heads,
peeping women
in strappy dresses

& ass-huggin' bell
bottoms. The rhythm
hits you like a slow
punch. There's the DJ,

hunched over turn-
tables, leaving
his crates & crates
of vinyl; one hand

holding his head,
nodding in agreement
to the beats'
unbroken enthymatic

claims, the other
spinning moods
& vibes so intoxicating
you throw back

your gin & tonic
& head for the
dance floor. It's time
to lose yourself.

The whole city is
here swiveling
on a throb. You bounce
back & forth in

front of speakers
stacked like blocks to
heaven. The dance floor's
a warm sky when

a woman joins your cipher.
Her eyes roll black,
vinyl-like. Inside you, so
many thresholds to find.

from *Erie*

MAJOR JACKSON

1.

I put a premium on rhymes—how could I
   Not living the times of the Supa
Emcees where styles are def, lyrics fly,
   Tight the way our minds move over
   Beats and grooves. Our brain matter's
Amped, mic-checked so we non-stop.
My spirit feels echoes thanks to hip-hop.

2.

I thought to send a note to 2Pac,
   Then wondered if he is there with you. Rumor
Has it he's far from dead,—that in fact
   He lives like Assata in Cuba
   Having fled Death Row. His mask consumes us
Still. A rapper shot, a martyr is born.
Sad not the man but an image we mourn:

3.

Party pack tight shots of supersized flesh
   While laughing, sucker-punched to dance,
Each cameo recording resurrects
   Pool-side queries, "How could I just kill a man?"
   An empire croons, toughed-up in a trance.
Imperialism rotates heavy as the world follows
Our nation's mantra: "clothes, bankrolls, and hoes."

4.

Paradise is a checkpoint of virgins
    For which a chest of bombs body-strapped
Blasts shrapnel eyes into martyrdom.
    So they tell us a river of honey maps
    Fluted glasses of desire. On a raft
Float children of Columbine and Palestine,
Bypassing their lives for an ocean of wine.

5.

A cafeteria was all one needed:
    A beat-box firm as the heart. We'd begin
A flow, spitting rhymes that superseded
    Our teacher's verdict: dim-witted children
    Who'll never taste marchand de vin.
Rap's dawning was the earth's reality,
To give a sound to a collective necessity.

6.

Couched in that "We" of the Real always
    Keeping it, that cool defiance, that
Organic e-mail to oppression, hallway
    Leanings and attitudinal grace, that
    Much future you heard, that
Sugar on the Hill ganging up airways,
Those Public Enemy freedom phrases,

7.

Those Boogie Down and Big Daddy
   Kanes, those Digable Planets & Afro
Names, that Rakim and Mr. Eric B
   Or Disposable Heroes of Hiphoprisy,
   That Salt N Pepa & Roxanne Roxanne,
West coast Coolio and fisted X-Clans,
Those Questing Tribes spitting *Concertos*

8.

Of the Desperadoes, but the Boom Bap's done
   Gone *Jiggy*, and every other word is *Ho*
Or *Niggy. Nicca:* still all the same, one
   Frame of the nation that spells hun-
   Ger, like a straw to the brain, video poison
Normalizes the game, our children pointing guns.
We need life like the Fugees need Lauryn.

This Beat Is Technotronic: A 90s Mixtape

ALLISON JOSEPH

Before the night is over, strike it up
like a black box. Ace of my own bass,

I saw the sign, boom shake the room
until you do what you like, hip-hop

hooray the daily currency. Take me
to another land because whatever

the scenario, I want to be there,
naughty by nature, not cause I hate you

but because I love you, now that we've
found love, heavy and sexy, too sexy

for this poem, for everybody, everybody.
Kiss me and I'll kiss you back, but you

ought to know it takes a nation of millions
to hold us back while doing the butt,

the sweat, the Humpty Dance and New
Jack Swing. Some think that we can't

flow, but we've got three as our magic
number, 3 feet high and rising higher,

past our own arrested development,
our tribe always on that quest for

that thing that thing that thing
that kills us softly—two times—

so we can rise again: no
scrubs, no diggity, no doubt.

Schadenfreude

Eli Karren

Laura says Drake and Taylor should fall in love
just so they can break up. Is it fucked up
that I want celebrity couples to exist just so
they can stop existing? *Imagine the songs,* she cackles,
and I can hear the beats, quivering in the cold,
unable to light their own cigarettes, their voices
like raccoons caught in Have-a-Heart traps.
I imagine Grammy season like some Wimbledon
for disassembled aortas, the crowd menacing as blood
stains the clay. Are we not entertained
with our voyeurism yet? It's not like there is a measure
for the purity of heartbreak. Imagine Taylor Swift
painted up like Marilyn Manson, studded and fanged,
her guitars sounding like the love child of a food processor
and a dial up signal. Why do I imagine her pain being feral?
Why do I want her eyes like satanic stained glass,
her lips dripping coyote blood? Why do I yearn
for Drake to grow a sensitive Robin Williams beard?
For him to only play mountain man cyphers, some Woody
Guthrie chopped over 808s? I want to stumble across him
on the Appalachian trail, playing Bon Iver around a campfire.
Hey Skinny Love, you don't have to do this to yourself.
Just wait till we get home, we can do it to each other.
No, I want Drake playing Microphones covers,
some Mount Eerie, I want him lamenting Geneviève.
I want him building an island in West Virginia,
somewhere the Tennessee Valley Authority hasn't electrified
yet. We only like Faustian myths because losing something
reminds us there is something to lose. Laura tells me
other people's comfort keeps her up at night,
that nothing disgusts her more than happy endings.

Dog Chapel

Eli Karren

My brother acts like he was the one who discovered hip-hop,
some brave new world bleeding out in the claw foot tub,
the tangerine tile floor & crimson bath mat. He says Suge Knight
blew its brains out on Hollywood Boulevard, that a ghetto

blaster peeled its skin from its face, some High EQ cut it down
like a Shaolin sword. One thing is for sure, he says, hip-hop isn't

dead like Rock & Roll is dead. Remember Kurt Cobain?
His blonde toes juggling a shotgun trigger, begging for reverb
& feedback. Think about hip-hop, how it strutted into gluttony
& withered with diabetes. My brother sounds like Mahler

all worked up over Stravinsky's ostinatos. He sounds like
he doesn't understand the *Rite of Spring* doesn't bloom in winter.

So, I tell him, no one really dies, because it's easier than saying art
isn't born. It metastasizes. Wouldn't this be better if it were about
   Tupac,

faking his death and selling condos in Somalia, about Elvis
being an extra in *Home Alone*? I, too, want an America

where Bankroll Fresh ghost-rides through the afterlife,
begging senators to change their positons on firearms. Hip-hop
never wanted to be Hard Rock, never asked Etheridge Knight to
   write
the final sixteen bars. It just wants to plead for peace, for Ice T

to be the punchline to a John Mulaney joke, for Xhibit to stop
needing to put diamond-studded deep fryers in the backs of
   Honda Civics.

Hip-hop just wants to die where my brother was born, wants
   some land

upstate, wants Snoop Dogg's ashes spread near the Dog
   Chapel,
some Mickey's poured over red clover and sycamore leaves,
while some boxers and poodles gallivant in the grass, barking
   at stillness.

the break

NATE MARSHALL

       is the place in the funk record
everybody goes crazy. if the dj is smart
the break is built longer. the break is hip-hop.

Grandmaster Flash took the break,
stretched the break. pulled it apart
like silly putty, plastered the party in it.

the break is where the drums take center
stage. the break is the center. the break
is the party. the break is built
from thrown-out equipment,
unused grooves. the break is struggle.

the break is the place
your sister doesn't have.
the break is the eviction.
the break is moving
back in with Moms.

the break is the break-
up. the break is garbage
bags of your sister's
belongings you find
in your room the day you
come back from summer camp.

the break is the party
you want to have
for your sister. the break
is your sister not being
only yours anymore.

your niece is the break.
the job applications
are the break. listening
to Lil' Kim & Biggie
while your sister braids
your niece's hair is the break.

the break is the job
your sister hates.

the break is the apartment hunt.
the arguments between Moms
& your sister. the break,
the apartment coming through.
the break, garbage bags
absent from your room.

Beat Boxing

for c-Lux

ADRIAN MATEJKA

That was the day the breakers started breaking & somebody broke
      the radio while snatching a sack of groceries from an old lady.
      That was the day the paper sack broke & granny smiths

& dry spaghetti spilled on the street like the words spoking a drunk's
free style. The inscription on the noodle box: this beat came up

      the sidewalk spacewalking the throat's feedback. This beat

loaned voice muscle instead of bringing the knuckle. The rappers rap
when this shows up. The breakers break
          when this shows up. This beat huffed
a mad circle of knuckle-ups. It breathed deep in someone else's
   crushing
dactylic and blinged hexameter where the handclap should be. This beat

cyphered gunshots into a Kangol dialectic. Empty grocery bags
   between
      handclaps. Old lady's wig between backslaps. Out of breath,
      this beat stuttered without applause like a loan shark on Thursday.

      Nobody else breathed as this beat made metronomes from breaths.

The old lady went inside & nobody breathed as a green apple rolled
to a bruising stop. The last beatless day ever. The last circle
of rhymes before cops sirened the block like it was Odysseus.

Wheels of Steel

ADRIAN MATEJKA

I got me two songs instead of eyes—
all swollen and blacked out

like the day after a lost fight. Two
jigsaws spinning, buzzing the backdrop

for woodshop or emcee, bar mitzvah
or afterset. *It's DJ Run, DMC rocking*

without a band, but not without me.
I make it rain. I make it rain on these

shined up rims still spinning after the car
stops. Dubs kind of grind like me

in their perpetuity. I'm the Wizard
of Oz if Oz was a fish fry in July.

Call me Master of the Cracked Fingers.
One song spins forward, the other

back to repeat itself: *Every day I'm*
hustlin'. Every day I'm hustlin'. Baby,

I'm the layaway payment on a Ferris
wheel. My songs orbit parking lots

and rent parties like the crazy lady's
eyes when she finds out her lover man

already left . . . *It's all because of you,*
I'm feeling sad and blue. One of my songs

spins backward, while the other plays
forward like sugar mixing in to make

the grape. My joints are the pinwheels
in this parade of moonwalks and uprocks:

See, I like to get down, Jack.

Tyndall Armory

ADRIAN MATEJKA

Public Enemy had no idea of what
to do on a stage in 1987, but we
didn't know what to do as rap crowd either.
Attendance was mandatory, jammed
into the Tyndall Armory, one night
after amateur boxing and one night
before bingo. A bunch of homeboys
kenti-ed together with African medallions,
graffiti spray-painted jeans—all of us
mad at the conspiracy of conspiracy,
staring each other down with a circular
anger only black men can justify.
Terminator X—his one-handed power
fist cut-and-scratch already perfected—
was the only thing keeping the crowd
from getting started. Bass lines, warning
sirens transformed into samples refusing
the Wop like the black maitre d'
at the Highlands Country Club refused
to seat black people. My friend Richard
was determined to be the first black
president, refused wine coolers and weed,
white women and white lines because
the Man could hold anything against him
during a campaign. As president,
he would buy Highlands and turn it into
a black thing. Terminator X had Rich
ready to say *peace* to the presidency
and Nat Turner the first patch of white
he saw. And when Chuck D mugged
the stage, African medallion swinging

like left hooks, baseball cap pulled down
so low his eyes were the idea of eyes,
the heat in that room was enough to make
any Tom reconsider his friendships.

This One's on the One

. . . the one about me

ADRIAN MATEJKA

What lovely backyards
in the neighborhood
of crossing over: *keeping*

it real a music, stick-pinned
to the marrow. Somebody
else's business can't be held

accountable for the skin's
synthesis, for fox fur coats,
chicken and orange juice

with starlets, or the inevitable
sunlight shaft from the recording
company. Music business,

sweet disinterested landmark.
Great emulsifier, eraser
for the pencil's half-steps.

Smoother of aphasia, sun dial
for all things slang and giggly.
Schiele sunflower in the eye

of the beholder. When
was the last time someone
said *the one about me* outside

of music's raw and remixed
context without smoothing
sideburns and eyebrows into

a couture of pimp-gaminess?
Next the nose's corners, rankles
up like a holy roller passing

a bar. How easily selfish
things transcribe themselves
over rock 'em sock 'em

beats. Q-Tip, you've created
a mosh pit of throwback
jerseys and soul patches pointing

out *happy* and *has-been*
for a crowd who ain't hearing it.
Like Chinese sign-language

of Joni Mitchell's voice.
Like explaining why your record
fancifully spins in the warp.

Pimp Limp

for Flava Flav, circa 1993

ADRIAN MATEJKA

On *Flavor of Love*, you crowed:
Your man Flava Flav's a pimp.
P-I-M-P! from the balcony.
A cascade of kiss and tell
on the woman walking in weaved
shame past the pool: head bowed,
bra tucked in armpit, heels clicking
maestro quick as early morning
sunbathers peeped upward
from behind sunglasses wondering
who disguised a lawn jockey
in a silk robe. It didn't have
to be this way. Fifteen years ago,
you took a jet-setting break once
a month to visit one of your girlfriends
in Bloomington. Me and my boys
hating on you before there was a name
for hateration. Before a football
player's overtures finally pried
that woman loose from your clocked
embrace. The time she cut you loose,
you came to town in a limousine
on a doughnut with a dented back
door. It was sunny, and you got
out of that limping car
with a matching limp to the applause
of me and my boys laughing.
You put your Gazelles on,
kissed two jeweled peace fingers
and tossed them to the crowd.

Poetry Suite for Karriem Riggins

JESSICA CARE MOORE

we. the infatuated undertow
born below the curved straight
line. cracked keys. somehow
finding the beautiful black

white noise in outer space hands
it's difficult to explain ourselves i see you.
i hear you. speaking the language of angels
the luxury of the double tongued
magic water people. a memory
a turn of your head. finds a smile
right above the water. just a few feet to find
breath. tar. wood. a shore. a safe place
to build music from tears.
the entire world inside one face.
nice to meet you. again.
we keep meeting our past
we keep running into our reflection
introductions are a drowning exit
& we don't teach our children to swim

this is above sea level

i see you. i hear you.
coming up for air. adjusting the headphones.
finding your tribe. a quick what up doe

a quiet corner exchange is testimony
is the yes yes ya'll
coded hellos. motor city steel.
still, there are flowers growing
from inside the empty.

crawfish voodoo & our fathers wishes
made this beat. this bottled spirit. this bread.
never broken. fed our families.
on the rocks. hand clap. sound.
rim shot. ice stories. drinking sugarcane
detroit rain. hits your forehead
finds your neck. when there is
nothing left. we the rooftop deck
the cross into. the ever after railroad.

the river of crystal currents.
the solo walk to heaven. the dobb
hat. the master. class. the vinyl moon
lighting up the sky. this room is
a constellation of notes & clocks
the 4am door knock.

it never leaves your body
simplicity is so complex.

just swim toward the compass
find your way to corner store prophets
the suite is always waiting
no keys necessary just
slide your delicate fingers
across my ribcage
push your head above the wave
tilt it back slowly
with a cool too real
to be magic

show them your colors your majesty
your honesty. your fearlessness.

your head nod

then keep going till they can't find your
sound in this atmosphere.

Ode to the Crossfader

JOHN MURILLO

Got this mixboard itch
    This bassline lifted
from my father's dusty
    wax   Forty crates stacked
in the back of the attic
    This static in the head-
phones   Hum in the blood
    This deep-bass buckshot
thump in the chest   Got
    reasons and seasons
pressed to both palms
    Two coins from each
realm   This memory
    Memory crossfaded and
cued   These knuckles'
    nicks and nightsweat
rites   This frantic
    abacus of scratch   Got
blood in the crates
    in the chest   in the dust
Field hollers to break-
    beats   My father's dusty
wax   My father's dust
    got reasons   Got night-
sweats and hollers
    pressed to both palms
breakbeats and hollers
    pressed to both palms
Static in the attic   Stacked
    crates of memory   Dust

blood and memory   Cross-
    faded and   Bass Cross-
faded and   cued   Crossfaded
    and   Static   Stacked hollers
Got reasons in the dust
    in the chest   Got seasons
in the blood   in the head-
    phones' hum   This deep-
bass   buckshot   blood
    pressed   to both palms
My father's dust   Pressed
    to both palms   Got
reasons and reasons
    and reasons

1989

John Murillo

There are no windows here, and the walls
Are lined with egg cartons. So if we listen
Past the sampled piano, drum kick
And speakerbox rumble, we'd still not hear
The robins celebrating daybreak.
The engineer worries the mixboard,
Something about a hiss lurking between notes.
Dollar Bill curses the engineer, time
We don't have. Says it's just a demo
And doesn't need perfecting. "Niggas
Always want to make like Quincy Jones
When you're paying by the hour."
Deejay Eddie Scizzorhandz—because he cuts
So nice—taps ashes into an empty pizza box,
Head nodding to his latest masterpiece:
Beethoven spliced with Mingus,
Mixed with Frankie Beverly, all laid
On Billy Squire's "Big Beat."
I'm in a corner, crossing out and rewriting
Lines I'll want to forget years later,
Looking up every now and then,
To watch Sheik Spear, Pomona's finest emcee,
In the vocal booth, spitting rhymes
He never bothers putting to paper,
Nearly hypnotized by the gold-plated cross
Swinging from his neck as he, too,
Will swing, days from now, before
They cut him from the rafters of a jail cell.

Kanye West to Angel Nafis on the Eve of Her Almost Non-Graduation from High School

ANGEL NAFIS

You gotta be the best. See that GPA? See
that stack of unfinished (late) worksheets?
That's not dope. That's not freshness. That's
worse than whack. If you got a big brain, and your heart
like, tremendous. If you ahead of your time, you know?
Ahead of THE times. Then basically you need to be
graduating from high school. I'm not saying everybody
gotta graduate from high school, or college, or like,
gotta get they diploma. But if you working towards something?
If you in the middle of a job, a grind, a project, whatever
and you can't even finish? You not excelling.
There's no life there. That's not a farm for a genius.
You can quit school, but when you not excelling
and school quits you? That's basically average.
Average is like a death. That's basically worse
than total failure. It dishonors the gold in you.
You gotta be golden. When Mr. Hunter waited
for two hours for you after school—for that independent
study you designed—and you ain't show up?
How you never showed up, after the first session,
where you read him a poem about your dad's
other kids, and y'all both cried. You're gonna wonder
how you graduated at all? You're gonna be afraid to open
your report card. And when you finally do you'll see your D.
A passing grade. He'll pass you. And you did no work.
You put in no work. You shed tears and kept it moving.
You didn't do your best. When you not doing your best—
fuck it—when you not *better* than your best, you turning

yourself into a liar. Your whole shit fraudulent.
You juggling with fragile material. You grabbing at
disappearing fabric. Like, that time Ms. Johnson called you
at your house, a week before today and told you
she thought you were a different kind of kid she thought
you had it. And you lied to her then, right through the phone,
on a Tuesday afternoon. You wanted her to think your problems
were bigger than they were. And they were.
They were humongous. Bigger than you knew.
And they was just beginning.

Please Wait (Or, There Are More Beautiful Things Than Beyoncé)

MORGAN PARKER

Please wait to record *Love Jones* at 8:48 Saturday on BET
Until your life is no longer defined by Beyoncé
Ants crawling over fallen leaves and little pieces of dog shit
Empty chicken boxes glowing with the remembrance of grease
There are more beautiful things than Beyoncé: self-awareness,
Leftover mascara in clumps, recognizing a pattern
That is for all the grown women out there
Whose countries hate them and their brothers
Who carry knives in their purses down the street
Maybe they will not get out alive
Maybe they will turn into air or news or brown flower petals
There are more beautiful things than Beyoncé:
Lavender, education, becoming other people,
The fucking sky
It's so overused because no one's sure of it
How it floats with flagrant privilege
And feels it can ask any question
Every day its ego gets bigger and you let that happen
But one day your shit will be unbelievably together
One day you'll care a whole lot you'll always take vitamins
And exercise without bragging and words will fit perfectly
Into your mouth like an olive soaked in gin
The glory of an olive soaked in gin & its smooth smallness
A gloss will snowfall onto your cheeks, the top of your lip
The sidewalks will be the same, evidenced
Combing your records you'll see the past and think OK
Once I was a different kind of person

B-Boy Infinitives

PATRICK ROSAL

To suck until our lips turned blue
the last drops of cool juice
from a crumpled cup sopped
with spit the first Italian Ice of summer
To chase popsicle stick skiffs
along the curb skimming stormwater
from Woodbridge Ave to Old Post Road
To be To B-boy To be boys who
snuck into a garden to pluck
a baseball from mud and shit
To hop that old man's fence before
he bust through his front door
with a lame-bull limp charge
and a fist the size of half a spade
To be To B-boy To lace shell-toe Adidas
To say Word to Kurtis Blow
To laugh the afternoons
someone's mama was so black
when she stepped out of the car
the oil light went on
To count hairs sprouting
around our cocks To touch
ourselves To pick the half-smoked
True Blues from my father's ash tray
and cough the gray grit
into my hands To run
my tongue along the lips of a girl
with crooked teeth To be
To B-boy To be boys for the ten days
an 8-foot gash of cardboard lasts

after we dragged that cardboard
seven blocks then slapped it
on the cracked blacktop To spin
on our hands and backs To bruise
elbows wrists and hips To Bronx-Twist
Jersey version beside the mid-day traffic
To swipe To pop To lock freeze and
drop dimes on the hot pavement—
even if the girls stopped watching
and the street lamps lit buzzed all
night we danced like that
and no one called us home

A Scavenger's Ode to the Turntable
(Or a Note to Thomas Alva Edison)

PATRICK ROSAL

We learned to poise pennies on the cartridge head
    so the diamond stylus would sit deep

in the vinyl's groove. A dance floor could fizz
    out quick if a record skipped when we spun back

the wax to its cue. Me and my boys, sons
    of cops, bookkeepers, and ex-priests, stayed awake

from noon to noon, excavating from crates
    some forgotten voice or violin to scratch.

We practiced thumbing the cheap dime-sized
    pitch controls and when those broke we didn't

just throw them out. Like the one Pingry prep-school
    kid who upgraded to a shiny six-channel model

(three-band eq and 12-bit sampling) and threw out
    his year-old Numark which we picked out of the garbage

and hoisted home. After fourteen screws,
    the top panel popped off and we plucked out

the pristine fader for transplant. We lifted
    the turntable's precious arm first,

then the platter. We pulled free the belt,
    and unscrewed the plastic top. I didn't take shop

or build a whole lot by hand, but I was good
    with a knife when I needed. I could poke the point

of a half-dull blade clean and gentle through
    the eighth-inch plastic and saw my way down

four inches, straight as I could make it, to pop into place
    the slider we harvested from the rich kid's rig.

I re-soldered the wires to the turntable pitch contacts.
    We did this in the basement of a maple split in Edison,

New Jersey, while our mothers played mahjong
    in the sala, and our fathers bet slow horses

and the government bombed Iraq. We juggled
    and chirped. We perfected the grind of a kick

and dropped it on the downbeat coming around.
    Half trash, half hallelujah. Our hands could cut

Bach to Bambataa and make a dance hall jump.
    It was our job to keep one ear to the backbeat

and the other to a music that no one else could hear.
    Out of a hunk of rescued junk, we built a machine

to mix our masters. We chopped up classics
    and made the whole block bounce.

For Tupac Amaru Shakur

Sonia Sanchez

who goes there? who is this young man born lonely?
who walks there? who goes toward death
whistling through the water
without his chorus? without his posse? without his song?

it is autumn now
in me autumn grieves
in this carved gold of shifting faces
my eyes confess to the fatigue of living.

i ask: does the morning weep for the dead?
i ask: were the bullets conscious atoms entering his chest?
i ask: did you see the light anointing his life?

the day i heard the sound of your death, my brother
i walked outside in the park
we your mothers wanted to see you safely home.
i remembered the poems in your mother's eyes as she
panther-laced warred against the state;
the day you became dust again
we your mothers held up your face green with laughter
and i saw you a child again outside your mother's womb

picking up the harsh handbook of Black life;
the day you passed into our ancestral rivers,
we your mothers listened for your intoxicating voice:
and i heard you sing of tunes bent back in a
cold curse against black
     against black (get black)
     against black (get black)

we anoint your life
in this absence
we anoint our tongues

with your magic. your genius.
casual warrior of sound
rebelling against humiliation
　　ayyee–ayyee–ayyee–
　　i'm going to save these young niggaz
　　because nobody else want to save them.
　　nobody ever came to save me . . . .

your life is still warm
on my breath, brother Tupac
Amaru Shakur
and each morning as i
pray for our people
navigating around these
earth pornographers
and each morning when
i see the blue tint of
our Blackness in the
morning dawn
i will call out to you again:

where is that young man born lonely?
and the ancestors' voices will reply:
he is home tattooing his skin with
white butterflies.

and the ancestors will say:
he is traveling with the laughter of trees
his reptilian eyes opening between the blue spaces.

and the ancestors will say:
why do you send all the blessed ones home early?
and the ancestors will say:
you people. Black. lost in the memory of silence.

look up at your children
joined at the spine with death and life.
listen to their genius in a season of dry rain.
listen to them chasing life falling
down getting up in this
house of blue mourning birds.

listen.
& he says: i ain't mad at ya
& we say: so dont cha be mad at yo self
& he says: me against the world
& we say: all of us against the world
& he says: keep yo head up
& we say: yeah family keep yo head up every day
& he says: dear mama, i love you
& we say: dear all the mamas we love you too
& he says: all eyez on me
& we say: kai fi African (come here African)
            all eyez on ya from the beginning of time
            from the beginning of time
            resist.
            resist.
            resist.
can you say it? resist. resist. resist.
can you say it? resist. resist. resist.
i say. can you do it? resist. resist. resist.
can you rub it into yo sockets? bones?
can you tattoo it on yo body?
so that you see, feel it strengthening you
as you cough blood before the world.

yeah. that's right. write it on your
forehead so you see yourselves as you walk past tomorrow
on your breasts so when
your babies suckle you, when your man woman

taste you they drink the milk of resistance. hee hee hee
take it inside you so when your lover. friend.
companion. enters you they are covered
with the juices, the sweet
cream of resistance. hee hee hee
make everyone who touches this mother lode
a lover of the idea of resistance.
can you say it? RESIST.
can you say it? RESIST.

til it's inside you and you resist
being an electronic nigger hating yo self & me
til you resist lying & gossiping & stealing &
killing each other on every saturday nite corner
til you resist having a baby cuz you want
something to love young sister. love yo self
til you resist being a shonuff stud fuckin
everything in sight, til you resist raping
yo sister, yo wife, somebody's grandmother.
til you resist recolonizing yo mind
mind mind mind mind

                resist
                resist
                resist for Tupac
                resist for you & me
                reSIST RESIST RESIST
                for Brother
                Tupac
                Amaru
                Shakur

cue the gangsta rap when my knees bend

after angel nafis

Danez Smith

because my mouth is a whip
& other times my mouth is a whip, you know

bass, rubber, leather seats, detailed flame
you know, some comfy, show-offy shit

fit for music. because he whips me
around easy as Sunday, no church

or plate to get to, just cruise, just eight
oh, eight inches of tar

for me to glide & boom. because it's a drug
& always violence & we hood all day

because my head bob the same, my spit be ready
to brawl. because the song need to have claws

& I need to ravage or revenge, either will do
what difference does a vowel make,

the only word my mouth cares for is O,
the only music the kind that bites.

C.R.E.A.M.

Danez Smith

after Morgan Parker, after Wu-Tang

in the morning I think about money
green horned lord of my waking
forest in which I stumbled toward no salvation
prison made of emerald & pennies
in my wallet I keep anxiety & a condom
I used to sell my body but now my blood spoiled
All my favorite songs tell me to get money
I'd rob a bank but I'm a poet
I'm so broke I'm a genius
If I was white, I'd take pictures of other pictures & sell them
I come from sharecroppers who come from slaves who do not come
from kings
sometimes I pay the weed man before I pay the light bill
sometimes is a synonym for often
I just want a grant or a fellowship or a rich white husband & I'll be
straight
I feel most colored when I'm looking at my bank account
I feel most colored when I scream *ball so hard motherfuckas wanna
find me*
I spent one summer stealing from ragstock
If I went to jail I'd live rent-free but there is no way to avoid making
white people richer
A prison is a plantation made of
stone & steel
Being locked up for selling drugs = Being locked up for
trying to eat
a bald fade cost 20 bones now a days
what's a blacker tax than blackness?
what cost more than being American
and poor?

here is where I say *reparations.*

here is where I say *got 20 bucks I can borrow?*

student loans are like slavery but not but with vacation days
but not but police

I don't know what it says about me when white institutions give me
money

how much is the power ball this week?

I'mma print my own money and be my own god and live forever in
a green frame

my grandmamma is great at saving money

before my grandfather passed he showed me where he hid
his money & his gun

my aunt can't hold on to a dollar, a job, her brain

I love how easy it is to be bad with money

don't ask me about my taxes

the b in debt is a silent black boy trapped

Hip-Hop Ghazal

Patricia Smith

Gotta love us brown girls, munching on fat, swinging blue hips,
decked out in shells and splashes, Lawdie, bringing them woo hips.

As the jukebox teases, watch my sistas throat the heartbreak,
inhaling bassline, cracking backbone and singing thru hips.

Like something boneless, we glide silent, seeping 'tween floorboards,
wrapping around the hims, and *ooh wee*, clinging like glue hips.

Engines grinding, rotating, smokin', gotta pull back some.
Natural minds are lost at the mere sight of ringing true hips.

Gotta love us girls, just struttin' down Manhattan streets
killing the menfolk with a dose of that stinging view. Hips.

Crying 'bout getting old—Patricia, you need to get up off
what God gave you. Say a prayer and start slinging. Cue hips.

Love Letter to Flavor Flav

Marcus Wicker

> *We know that we are beautiful. And ugly too.*
> —Langston Hughes

I think I love you.
How you suck fried chicken grease
off chalkboard fingers, in public!
Or walk the wrong way down an escalator
with a clock around your neck.
How you rapped about the poor
with a gold-tooth grin.
How your gold teeth spell your name.
How you love your name is beautiful.
You shout your name 100 times each day.
They say, if you repeat something enough
you can become it. I'd like to know:
Does *Flavor Flaaav!* sound ugly to you?
I think it's slightly beautiful.
I bet you love mirrors.
Tell the truth,
when you find plastic Viking horns
or clown shade staring back,
is it beauty that you see?
Or Vaudeville?
To express myself honestly enough;
that, my friend, is very hard to do.
Those are Bruce Lee's words.
I mention Bruce Lee here, only
because you remind me of him.
That's a lie. But your shades do
mirror a mask he wore
as Green Hornet's trusty sidekick.
No, I'm not calling names.
Chuck D would have set cities on fire

had you let him.
You were not Public Enemy's sidekick.
You hosed down whole crowds
in loud-mouth flame retardant spit.
You did this only by repeating your name.
Flavor Flaaav! Flavor Flaaav!
I think I love you. I think I really might
mean it this time.
William. Can I call you William?
I should have asked 27 lines ago:
What have you become?
How you've lived saying nothing
save the same words each day
is a kind of freedom or beauty.
Please, tell me I'm not lying to us.

Expecting

KEVIN YOUNG

Grave, my wife lies back, hands cross
her chest, while the doctor searches early
for your heartbeat, peach pit, unripe

plum—pulls out the world's worst
boom box, a Mr. Microphone, to broadcast
your mother's lifting belly.

The whoosh and bellows of mama's body
and beneath it: nothing. Beneath
the slow stutter of her heart: nothing.

The doctor trying again to find you, fragile
fern, snowflake. Nothing.
After, my wife will say, in fear,

impatient, she went beyond her body,
this tiny room, into the ether—
for now, we spelunk for you one last time

lost canary, miner of coal
and chalk, lungs not yet black—
I hold my wife's feet to keep her here—

and me–trying not to dive starboard
to seek you in the dark water. And there
it is: faint, an echo, faster and further

away than mother's, all beat box
and fuzzy feedback. You are like hearing
hip-hop for the first time—power

hijacked from a lamppost—all promise.
You couldn't sound better, break-
dancer, my favorite song bumping

from a passing car. You've snuck
into the club underage and stayed!
Only later, much, will your mother

begin to believe your drumming
in the distance—my Kansas City
and Congo Square, this jazz band

vamping on inside her.

Biographies

Kim Addonizio is the author of several books of poetry and prose. Her latest books are a poetry collection, *Mortal Trash* (W.W. Norton), and a memoir, *Bukowski in a Sundress: Confessions from a Writing Life* (Penguin).

Ai was the author of *Dread* (2003); *Vice: New and Selected Poems* (1999), which won the National Book Award for Poetry; and *Greed* (1993), among many other books. She received awards from the Guggenheim Foundation and the National Endowment for the Arts.

James Baldwin was an essayist, playwright, and novelist who penned such classic titles as *Go Tell It on the Mountain, Native Son,* and *Another Country.*

Amiri Baraka (born Everett LeRoi Jones) was an African-American writer of poetry, drama, fiction, and essays. He was the author of numerous books of poetry, including *Preface to a Twenty Volume Suicide Note, Black Magic,* and *Transbluesency: The Selected Poems of Amiri Baraka (LeRoi Jones).*

Tara Betts is the author of *Break the Habit* and *Arc & Hue.* She's a co-editor of *The Beiging of America: Personal Narratives about Being Mixed Race in the 21st Century* and editor of Philippa Duke Schuyler's long out-of-print memoir *Adventures in Black and White.* Her work has appeared in *Poetry, Essence, Nylon, Lit Hub,* and numerous anthologies. Tara is part of the MFA faculty at Chicago State University and Stonecoast at University of Southern Maine

Sarah Blake is the recipient of an NEA literature fellowship and author of the poetry collections *Let's Not Live on Earth* (2017), including the sci-fi epic "The Starship," and *Mr. West* (2015), an unauthorized biography of Kanye West. Her debut novel, *Naamah,* retells the story of the Great Flood from the perspective of Noah's wife (2019). Her writing appears in *Catapult, The Paris Review,* and *The Kenyon Review.*

Adrea Bogle lives in southwest Colorado where she works in special education. She has had poems published in *Brilliant Corners: A Journal of Jazz and Literature.*

Jim Carroll revised a diary he kept as a teenager into his most famous literary work, *The Basketball Diaries* (1978), which chronicles his double life as a star student and basketball player who was also a junkie. At sixteen he published his first book of poems, *Organic Trains* (1967). He published five more books of poetry, including *Living at the Movies* (1973), and *Fear of Dreaming* (1993).

Michael Cirelli is the author of several books of poems, including *The Grind* (2013). Cirelli is the executive director of Urban Word NYC, has been a National Poetry Slam finalist, and was featured on the HBO series Def Poetry Jam.

Wanda Coleman's collection *Bathwater Wine* (1998) received the 1999 Lenore Marshall Prize. Coleman received fellowships from the National Endowment for the Arts and the Guggenheim Foundation. Her books of poetry include *Mercurochrome: New Poems* (2001), which was a finalist for the National Book Award in poetry, *Native in a Strange Land: Trials & Tremors* (1996), and *Hand Dance* (1993). Coleman lived in Los Angeles until her death in 2013.

Billy Collins is the author of several books of poetry, including *Aimless Love: New and Selected Poems* (2013), *Horoscopes for the Dead: Poems* (2012); and *The Trouble with Poetry* (2005). He was poet laureate of the United States from 2001-2003.

Jayne Cortez's books of poetry include *On the Imperial Highway: New and Selected Poems* (2008), *The Beautiful Book* (2007), and *Jazz Fan Looks Back* (2002). Cortez also released a number of recordings, many with her band The Firespitters, including *Taking the Blues Back Home* (1997), *Cheerful & Optimistic* (1994), and *Everywhere Drums* (1991).

Kevin Coval is the author of over a dozen books, including the poetry book *A People's History of Chicago* and the play, *This is Modern Art*, co-written with Idris Goodwin. Coval is the editor of *The BreakBeat Poets*, the Artistic Director of Young Chicago Authors, & the founder of Louder Than a Bomb, the world's largest youth poetry festival. He is editor of BreakBeat Publishing, an imprint of Haymarket Books dedicated to publishing radically fresh voices.

Stephen Cramer's first book of poems, *Shiva's Drum*, was a winner of the 2003 National Poetry Series. *From the Hip*, which follows the history of hip hop in a series of 56 sonnets, came out in 2014. *Bone Music* (2016) won the 2015 Louise Bogan Award. His work has appeared in journals such as *The American Poetry Review, African American Review, The Yale Review,* and *Harvard Review*. An assistant poetry editor at *Green Mountains Review*, he teaches writing and literature at UVM.

Kyle Dargan is the author of five poetry collections, most recently *Anagnorisis* (TriQuarterly/Northwestern UP, 2018). He is currently an Associate Professor of literature and Assistant Director of creative writing at American University, as well as the founder and editor of *Post No Ills* magazine.

Toi Derricotte's sixth collections of poetry, *"I" New and Selected Poems*, was published in 2019 and shortlisted for the 2019 National Book Award. Other books of poetry include The Undertaker's Daughter, Tender, and Captivity. She also wrote the literary memoir *The Black Notebooks*, which won the Anisfield-Wolf Book Award for Non-Fiction and was a New York Times Notable Book of the Year. With Cornelius Eady, Derricotte co-founded the Cave Canem Foundation. She is Professor Emerita from University of Pittsburgh and a former Chancellor of the Academy of American Poets..

Joel Dias-Porter edited the anthology *The Black Rooster Social Inn* (1997). Dias-Porter's poetry has also been featured in the anthologies *Bum Rush the Page: A Def Poetry Jam* (2001) and *Catch the Fire!!!: A Cross-Generational Anthology of Contemporary African-American Poetry* (1998), on the *Today Show*, and in the documentaries *Voices Against Violence* and *SlamNation*, as well as the feature film *Slam*. A Cave Canem Fellow and member of Washington DC's WriterCorps, Porter has taught at Duke Ellington School of the Performing Arts.

Mark Doty is the author of several collections of poetry, including *Deep Lane* (2015), *Fire to Fire: New and Selected Poems* (2008), which received the National Book Award, *Source* (2002), and *Sweet Machine* (1998). *My Alexandria* (1993) was chosen by Philip Levine for the National Poetry Series. Doty has received fellowships from the Guggenheim Foundation, the National Endowment for the Arts, the Rockefeller Foundation, and the Whiting Foundation.

Rita Dove served as Poet Laureate of the United States from 1993 to 1995 and as Poet Laureate of the Commonwealth of Virginia from 2004 to 2006. She has received numerous literary and academic honors, among them the 1987 Pulitzer Prize in Poetry and the 1996 National Humanities Medal from President Clinton. In 2006 she received the Common Wealth Award of Distinguished Service, and in 2009 she received the Fulbright Lifetime Achievement Medal. She has published the poetry collections *The Yellow House on the Corner* (1980), *Museum* (1983), *Thomas and Beulah* (1986), *Grace Notes* (1989), *Selected Poems* (1993), *Mother Love* (1995), *On the Bus with Rosa Parks* (1999), *American Smooth* (2004), and *Sonata Mulattica* (2009; winner of the Hurston/Wright Legacy Award).

Carol Ann Duffy's books of poetry include: *New & Collected Poetry for Children* (2009); *Rapture* (2006); *Selected Poems* (2004); and *Feminine Gospels* (2002). *Mean Time* (1993) won the Whitbread Poetry Award and the Forward Poetry Prize. She was appointed the poet laureate of Britain in 2009.

Thomas Sayers Ellis is the author of *Skin, Inc.* (2013), *The Maverick Room* (2005), and *Identity Repair Poems* (2010). He co-founded the Dark Room Collective in Cambridge, Massachusetts, and received a Whiting Award in 2005. Ellis has taught at Sarah Lawrence College, Case Western Reserve University, and Lesley University. He lives in Brooklyn, New York.

Sascha Feinstein's books include two poetry collections (*Misterioso* and *Ajanta's Ledge*), two memoirs (*Black Pearls: Improvisations on a Lost Year* and *Wreckage: My Father's Legacy of Art & Junk*), and a collection of interviews (*Ask Me Now: Conversations on Jazz & Literature*). In 1996, he founded *Brilliant Corners: A Journal of Jazz & Literature*, which he still edits. He is the Robert L. and Charlene Shangraw Professor of English at Lycoming College.

Krista Franklin is an interdisciplinary artist whose work appears in literary journals, anthologies, performances, and book projects, including *Poetry, Encyclopedia, Vol. F-K* and *L-Z, The Long Term*, and *The BreakBeat Poets*. She's the author of *Under the Knife* (Candor Arts, 2018) and *Study of Love & Black Body* (Willow Books, 2012). Her visual art has been published and exhibited widely.

Yolanda Franklin's work has appeared in *Sugar House Review, Crab Orchard Review*, and *The Hoot & Howl of the Owl Anthology of Hurston Wright Writers' Week*. She was nominated for a 2012 Pushcart Poetry Prize and was awarded a 2012 Cave Canem fellowship. Her collection of poems, *Southern Pout*, was a finalist for the 2011 Crab Orchard Series in Poetry Award. She is a graduate of Lesley University's MFA Writing Program.

Allen Ginsberg was one of the most influential writers in the Beat Generation. He was the author of over twenty books of poetry, including *Howl and Other Poems* and *Kaddish.*

Dana Gioia has published five full-length collections of poetry, most recently *99 Poems: New & Selected*. His collection *Interrogations at Noon* won the 2002 American Book Award. An influential critic, Gioia's 1991 volume *Can Poetry Matter?*, a finalist for the National Book Critics Circle award, helped to revive the role of poetry in American public culture.

Aracelis Girmay is the author of *Teeth* and *Kingdom Animalia*, which was a finalist for the National Book Critics Circle Award.

Albert Goldbarth has published more than twenty-five collections of poetry, including *To Be Read in 500 Years: Poems* (2009), *The Kitchen Sink: New and Selected Poems 1972-2007* (2007), and *Saving Lives* (2001).

Idris Goodwin is an award-winning poet, playwright, director and orator. He is the author of the Pushcart nominated essay collection *These Are The Breaks* and *Inauguration,* winner of the 2017 Literary Arts Award from The Pikes Peak Arts Council. His words have appeared on HBO,

Sesame Street, BBC radio and Discovery Channel. His widely produced plays include *How We Got On, Hype Man: a break beat play, And in This Corner: Cassius Clay* and *This Is Modern Art* co-written with Kevin Coval.

Thom Gunn's works include *Fighting Terms* (1954), *Jack Straw's Castle* (1976), *The Passages of Joy* (1982), *The Man With Night Sweats* (1992), *Shelf Life* (1993) and *Frontiers of Gossip* (1997).

Barbara Hamby: In 2010, Hamby's book of stories, *Lester Higata's 20th Century*, won the Iowa Short Fiction Prize/John Simmons Award, she was named a Distinguished University Scholar at Florida State, and she received a Guggenheim Fellowship. Her most recent books include *On the Street of Divine Love: New and Selected Poems*, and *All-Night Lingo Tango*.

Michael S. Harper published more than ten books of poetry, including *Dear John, Dear Coltrane* (1970), which was nominated for the National Book Award. His other collections include *Images of Kin* (1977), which won the Melville-Cane Award from the Poetry Society of America and was nominated for the National Book Award, and *History Is Your Heartbeat* (1971), which won the Black Academy of Arts & Letters Award for poetry.

Alysia Nicole Harris has a Ph.D. in linguistics from Yale University and an MFA in poetry from New York University.

Terrance Hayes is the author of *Lighthead* (2010), winner of the National Book Award. His other books include *American Sonnets for my Past and Future Assassin* (2018), *Wind in a Box* (2006), *Hip Logic* (2002), and *Muscular Music* (1999). His honors include a National Endowment for the Arts Fellowship, a Guggenheim Fellowship, and a MacArthur Fellowship. *How to Be Drawn* (2015) was a finalist for the 2015 National Book Award and the 2016 National Book Critics Circle Award.

Tony Hoagland's books of poetry include *Unincorporated Persons in the Late Honda Dynasty* (2010), *What Narcissism Means to Me* (2003), a finalist for the National Book Critics Circle Award, and *Donkey Gospel* (1998), which received the James Laughlin Award. Hoagland also received two grants from the National Endowment for the Arts, a fellowship to the Provincetown Fine Arts Work Center, as well as the Poetry Foundation's 2005 Mark Twain Award in recognition of his contribution to humor in American poetry.

Anna Claire Hodge teaches creative writing at the University of North Florida. Her work has appeared in *Prairie Schooner, Mid-American Review, Southern Indiana Review, Crab Orchard Review, Hayden's Ferry Review,* and others. Anna Claire's poems have been anthologized in *It Was Written: Poems Inspired by Hip-Hop* and *Best New Poets 2013.*

Chinaka Hodge is a poet, educator, playwright and screenwriter. In 2010, Hodge received USC's prestigious Annenberg Fellowship to continue her studies at its School of Cinematic Arts. She received her MFA in Writing for Film and TV in 2012. In the fall of that year, she received the SF Foundation's Phelan Literary Award for emerging Bay Area talent. Hodge was also a 2012 Artist in Residence at The Headlands Center for the Arts in Marin, CA.

Marie Howe's most recent book is *Magdalene. The Kingdom of Ordinary Time* (2009) was a finalist for the Los Angeles Times Book Prize. Her other collections of poetry include *What the Living Do* (1998) and *The Good Thief* (1988), which was selected by Margaret Atwood for the 1987 National Poetry Series.

Langston Hughes was an American poet, novelist, and playwright whose African-American themes made him a primary contributor to the Harlem Renaissance of the 1920s.

Lynda Hull's collections include *Ghost Money* (1986), recipient of the Juniper Prize, *Star Ledger* (1991), which won the 1991 Carl Sandburg and 1990 Edwin Ford Piper awards, and *The Only World: Poems*, published posthumously in 1995 and finalist for the National Book Critics Circle Award in Poetry. In 2006, Graywolf Press published her *Collected Poems*, edited by her husband, David Wojahn.

Angela Jackson is the author of numerous collections of poetry, including *VooDoo/Love Magic* (1974); *Dark Legs and Silk Kisses: The Beatitudes of the Spinners* (1993), which won the Carl Sandburg Award; and National Book Award–nominated *And All These Roads Be Luminous: Poems Selected and New* (1998). Her novel *Where I Must Go* (2009) won the American Book Award. Jackson's honors include a Pushcart Prize, the Poetry Society of America's Shelley Memorial Award, and a grant from the National Endowment for the Arts.

Major Jackson is an American poet, professor and the author of four collections of poetry: *Roll Deep* (2016), *Holding Company* (2010), and *Hoops* (2006), both finalists for an NAACP Image Award for Outstanding Literature-Poetry and *Leaving Saturn* (2002), winner of the 2001 Cave Canem Poetry Prize and finalist for a National Book Critics Award Circle. He is also a recipient of a Whiting Writers' Award and has been honored by the Pew Fellowship in the Arts and the Witter Bynner Foundation in conjunction with the Library of Congress.

David Jauss is the author of two books of poetry, *Improvising Rivers* and *You Are Not Here*; four books of fiction, including two volumes of new and selected stories, *Glossolalia* and *Nice People*; and the craft book *On Writing Fiction*. His poems have appeared in *Brilliant Corners, The Georgia Review, The Missouri Review, The Nation, The Paris Review, Ploughshares, Poetry, Shenandoah*, and numerous other journals and anthologies. He teaches in the MFA in Writing Program at Vermont College of Fine Arts.

Tyehimba Jess is the author of two books of poetry, *Leadbelly* and *Olio*. *Olio* won the 2017 Pulitzer Prize, the Anisfield-Wolf Book Award, The Midland Society Author's Award in Poetry, and received an Outstanding Contribution to Publishing Citation from the Black Caucus of the American Library Association. It was also nominated for the National Book Critics Circle Award, the PEN Jean Stein Book Award, and the Kingsley Tufts Poetry Award. *Leadbelly* was a winner of the 2004 National Poetry Series.

A. Van Jordan is the author of four collections: *Rise*, which won the PEN/Oakland Josephine Miles Award (2001); *M-A-C-N-O-L-I-A*, (2005), which was listed as one the Best Books of 2005 by the London Times; *Quantum Lyrics*, (2007); and *The Cineaste* (2013). Jordan has been awarded a Whiting Writers Award, an Anisfield-Wolf Book Award, and a Pushcart Prize. He is also the recipient of a John Simon Guggenheim Fellowship, and a United States Artists Fellowship. He is the Henry Rutgers Presidential Professor at Rutgers University-Newark.

Allison Joseph is the author of several poetry collections, including *Confessions of a Barefaced Woman* (2018); *Worldly Pleasures* (2004); and *What Keeps Us Here* (1992), winner of the John C. Zacharis First Book Award. Joseph has received fellowships and awards from the Illinois Arts Council. She teaches at and directs the Southern Illinois University–Carbondale MFA Program in Creative Writing, where she also serves as the editor-in-chief and poetry editor of *Crab Orchard Review*.

Julie Kane is a past National Poetry Series winner and Louisiana Poet Laureate. Her fifth book of poems, *Mothers of Ireland*, is forthcoming from LSU Press in 2020. Professor Emeritus of English at Northwestern State University of Louisiana, she currently teaches in the low-residency MFA program at Western Colorado University.

Jack Kerouac was an American writer best known for the novel *On the Road*, which became an American classic. He was a prominent member of the Beats in the 1950s.

Eli Karren, after braving many years in the frozen wilderness of New England, is now a resident of Austin, Texas. He graduated from the University of Vermont, where he won the Benjamin C. Wainwright Poetry Prize. His works have appeared in *Redlands Review, Vantage Point*, and *In Layman's Terms*.

Etheridge Knight's first volume of poetry was *Poems from Prison* (1968). After his release from prison, Knight taught at various universities and contributed to several magazines, working for two years as an editor of *Motive* and as a contributing editor of *New Letters* (1974). Much of his poetry was collected in *The Essential Etheridge Knight* (1986). He received honors from such institutions as the Guggenheim Foundation, the National Endowment for the Arts, and the Poetry Society of America.

Yusef Komunyakaa has published several books of poems, including *The Emperor of Water Clocks* (2015); *The Chameleon Couch* (2011); *Warhorses* (2008); *Taboo: The Wishbone Trilogy, Part 1* (2006); and *Pleasure Dome: New & Collected Poems, 1975-1999*. He received the Pulitzer Prize for *Neon Vernacular: New & Selected Poems 1977-1989* (1994).

Dorianne Laux's fifth collection, *The Book of Men*, winner of The Paterson Prize, is available from W.W. Norton. Her fourth book of poems, *Facts about the Moon*, won The Oregon Book Award and was short-listed for the Lenore Marshall Poetry Prize. Laux is also the author of *Awake*; *What We Carry*, a finalist for the National Book Critic's Circle Award; and *Smoke*. She is the co-author of *The Poet's Companion: A Guide to the Pleasures of Writing Poetry*.

Philip Levine published numerous books of poetry, including *News of the World* (2009); *Breath* (2004); *The Mercy* (1999); *The Simple Truth* (1994), which won the 1995 Pulitzer Prize; *What Work Is* (1991), which won the 1991 National Book Award.

Larry Levis's second book, *The Afterlife*, was a Lamont Poetry Selection by The Academy of American Poets. *The Dollmaker's Ghost* won the National Poetry Series. Other awards included a YM-YWHA Discovery award, three fellowships in poetry from the National Endowment for the Arts, a Fulbright Fellowship, and a Guggenheim Fellowship.

Nate Marshall is an editor of *The BreakBeat Poets: New American Poetry in the Age of Hip-Hop*. His first book, *Wild Hundreds*, won the Agnes Lynch Starrett Prize. His rap album *Grown* came out in 2015 with his group Daily Lyrical Product. He is a Visiting Assistant Professor at Wabash College. He received his MFA in Poetry at The University of Michigan where he also served as a Zell Postgraduate Fellow. A Cave Canem Fellow, his work has appeared in *Poetry, Indiana Review, The New Republic, Prairie Schooner*, and in many other publications.

Donna Masini's first collection of poems, *That Kind of Danger*, was selected by Mona Van Duyn for the Barnard Women Poet's Prize. Her second, *Turning to Fiction*, was published in 2004. *4:30 Movie* was published by W.W. Norton in 2018. Her work has appeared in journals and anthologies including *Best American Poetry 2015, Ploughshares*, and *APR*. A recipient of a National Endowment for the Arts Fellowship, New York Foundation for the Arts Grant, and a Pushcart Prize, she is an Associate Professor of English at Hunter College.

Adrian Matejka is the author of *The Devil's Garden* (Alice James Books, 2003), and *Mixology* (Penguin, 2009). *The Big Smoke* (Penguin, 2013) won the Anisfield-Wolf Book Award and was a finalist for the National Book Award and the Pulitzer Prize. His most recent collection, *Map to the Stars* (Penguin), was published in 2017. He is Poet Laureate of Indiana and teaches at Indiana University in Bloomington.

William Matthews published eleven books of poetry, including *Time & Money* (1996), which won the National Book Critics Circle Award and was a finalist for the Lenore Marshall Poetry Prize; *Selected Poems and Translations 1969-1991* (1992); *Blues If You Want* (1989). Collections published posthumously include *Search Party: Collected Poems*, edited by his son Sebastian Matthews and Stanley Plumly (2004), and *After All: Last Poems* (1998). He was also the author of a book of essays entitled *Curiosities* (1989).

jessica Care moore, the CEO of Moore Black Press, is the author of several works. Her first recording project, *Black Tea—The Legend of Jessi James*, was released in 2015 by Talib Kweli's Javotti Media.

Stanley Moss's first book of poems, *The Wrong Angel,* was published in 1966. Since then he has also published *The Skull of Adam* (1979), *The Intelligence of Clouds* (1989), *Asleep in the Garden* (1997), *A History of Color* (2003), *Songs of Imperfection* (2005), *New and Selected Poems* (2006), *Rejoicing* (2009), *God Breaketh Not All Men's Hearts Alike* (2011), *No Tear is Commonplace* (2013) and *It's About Time* (2015). In 1977, he founded Sheep Meadow Press, a non-profit publishing company that publishes poetry and belles lettres.

Lisel Mueller is the author of five books of poetry and is also a published translator. She won the National Book Award for *The Need to Hold Still* in 1981 and the Pulitzer Prize for *Alive Together: New and Selected Poems* in 1997.

Paul Muldoon was born in County Armagh in 1951. He now lives in New York. A former radio and television producer for the BBC in Belfast, he has taught at Princeton University for thirty years. He is the author of twelve collections of poetry including *Moy Sand and Gravel*, for which he won the 2003 Pulitzer Prize. His most recent book is *Selected Poems 1968-2014.*

John Murillo, an Afro-Chicano poet and playwright, is the current Jay C. and Ruth Halls Poetry Fellow at the Wisconsin Institute for Creative Writing. He is the author of the poetry collection, *Up Jump the Boogie* (2010) and the choreo-play, *TRIGGER*, which was commissioned by Edgeworks Dance Theater and is scheduled for production in early 2011. A graduate of New York University's MFA program in creative writing, he has also received fellowships from *The New York Times*, Cave Canem, and the Fine Arts Work Center in Provincetown, Massachusetts.

Angel Nafis is the author of *BlackGirl Mansion* (Red Beard Press, 2012). Her work has appeared in *The BreakBeat Poets Anthology, Buzzfeed Reader, The Rumpus, Poetry*, and more. She is the founder, curator, and host of the Greenlight Poetry Salon. She is a Cave Canem graduate fellow and the recipient of the 2016 Ruth Lily Dorothy Sargent Rosenberg Fellowship and the 2017 NEA Creative Writing Fellowship. With poet Morgan Parker she is The Other Black Girl Collective.

Idra Novey is the author of the novels *Those Who Knew* and *Ways to Disappear*. Her poetry collections include *Exit, Civilian*, winner of the National Poetry Series, and *The Next Country*. She has also translated the work of Brazilian poets Manoel de Barros and Paulo Henriques Britto.

Joyce Carol Oates's novels *Black Water* (1992) and *What I Lived For* (1994) were nominated for the Pulitzer Prize. The author of over 40 books, she is one of the most prolific authors out there. Her short stories have appeared in almost every issue of *Prize Stories: The O. Henry Awards* for the last forty years.

Frank O'Hara's *Meditations in an Emergency* (1956) and *Lunch Poems* (1964), are impromptu lyrics, a jumble of witty talk, journalistic parodies, and surrealist imagery. O'Hara worked at the Museum of Modern Art, where he curated exhibitions and wrote introductions and exhibit catalogs. On July 25, 1966, O'Hara was killed in a sand buggy accident on Fire Island. He was forty years old.

Morgan Parker is the author of *Other People's Comfort Keeps Me Up at Night*, which was selected by Eileen Myles for the 2013 Gatewood Prize. Her second collection, *There Are More Beautiful Things Than Beyoncé*, was published by Tin House Books in 2017. Parker's work has been featured in numerous publications, as well as anthologized in *Why I Am Not A Painter, The BreakBeat Poets: New American Poetry in the Age of Hip-Hop*, and *Best American Poetry 2016*. She is the winner of a 2016 Pushcart Prize and a Cave Canem graduate fellow.

David Rivard is the author of *Otherwise Elsewhere, Sugartown, Bewitched Playground, Wise Poison* (winner of the James Laughlin Prize and a finalist for the Los Angeles Times Book Award), and *Torque*, winner of the 1987 Agnes Lynch Starrett Poetry Prize. His poems and essays appear in the *American Poetry Review, TriQuarterly, Ploughshares, Poetry London*, and other magazines. Rivard has been awarded fellowships from the Guggenheim Foundation, the National Endowment for the Arts, and the Fine Arts Work Center in Provincetown.

Patrick Rosal's newest book is *Brooklyn Antediluvian* (2016). Previously, *Boneshepherds* (2011) was named a small press highlight by the National Book Critics Circle and a notable book by the Academy of American Poets. He is also the author of *My American Kundiman* (2006), and *Uprock Headspin Scramble and Dive* (2003). His collections have been honored with the Association of Asian American Studies Book Award, and the Asian American Writers Workshop Members' Choice Award. In 2009, he was awarded a Fulbright Fellowship to the Philippines.

Muriel Rukeyser published eighteen books of poetry, including *The Collected Poems of Muriel Rukeyser*. Her first book, *Theory of Flight*, won the Yale Series of Younger Poets Award in 1935.

Sonia Sanchez is the author of over 16 books. A recipient of a National Endowment for the Arts, the Lucretia Mott Award for 1984, the Outstanding Arts Award from the Pennsylvania Coalition of 100 Black Women, the Community Service Award from the National Black Caucus of State Legislators, she is a winner of the 1985 American Book Award for *Homegirls and Handgrenades. Does Your House Have Lions?* was a finalist for the National Book Critics Circle Award. She is the Poetry Society of America's 2001 Robert Frost Medalist.

Neil Shepard's latest book, *How It Is: Selected Poems*, was published in 2018 by Salmon Poetry (Ireland). His sixth and seventh books of poetry were published in 2015: *Hominid Up* (Salmon Poetry), and a full collection of poems and photographs, *Vermont Exit Ramps II* (Green Writers Press, Vermont). His poems appear in such magazines as the *Harvard Review, Paris Review, Southern Review*, and *Sewanee Review*. He founded *Green Mountains Review* and was senior editor for a quarter-century.

Betsy Sholl's ninth collection is *House of Sparrows: New & Selected Poems* (University of Wisconsin, 2019). Her eighth collection, *Otherwise Unseeable*, won the 2015 Maine Literary Award for Poetry. She was Poet Laureate of Maine from 2006 to 2011, and currently teaches in the MFA Program of Vermont College of Fine Arts. She occasionally performs with two jazz musicians who have arranged music to go with her poems.

Charles Simic is a poet, essayist and translator. He has published twenty books of his own poetry, seven books of essays, a memoir, and numerous books of translations of French, Serbian, Croatian, Macedonian, and Slovenian poetry for which he has received many literary awards, including the Pulitzer Prize, the Griffin Prize, the MacArthur Fellowship and Wallace Stevens Award from the Academy of American Poets. Simic was the Poet Laureate of the United States 2007-2008.

Danez Smith is a black, queer, poz writer and performer from St. Paul, MN. Smith is the author of *Don't Call Us Dead* (Graywolf Press, 2017), finalist for the National Book Award, and *[insert] boy* (YesYes Books, 2014), winner of the Kate Tufts Discovery Award and the Lambda Literary Award for Gay Poetry. Smith is a member of the Dark Noise Collective and is the co-host of VS with Franny Choi, a podcast sponsored by the Poetry Foundation and Postloudness. Smith's third collection, *Homie*, will be published by Graywolf in Spring 2020.

Patricia Smith is the author of six volumes of poetry, including *Shoulda Been Jimi Savannah* (winner of the 2014 Rebekah Bobbitt Prize from the Library of Congress, the 2013 Lenore Marshall Poetry Prize from the Academy American Poets and the Phillis Wheatley Award in Poetry), *Blood Dazzler* (a National Book Award finalist), and *Teahouse of the Almighty* (a National Poetry Series winner), all from Coffee House Press; *Close to Death* and *Big Towns, Big Talk,* both from Zoland Books; and *Life According to Motown* from Tia Chucha Press.

J.R. Solonche is the author of *Beautiful Day* (Deerbrook Editions), *Won't Be Long* (Deerbrook Editions), *Heart's Content* (Five Oaks Press), *Invisible, The Black Birch* (Kelsay Books), *I, Emily Dickinson & Other Found Poems* (Deerbrook Editions), *In Short Order* (Kelsay Books), *Tomorrow, Today & Yesterday* (Deerbrook Editions), and coauthor of *Peach Girl: Poems for a Chinese Daughter* (Grayson Books).

Lisa Russ Spaar teaches creative writing at the University of Virginia, where she is Professor of English and Director of the Creative Writing Program. She is the author of over ten books, most recently *Orexia: Poems* (Persea, 2017) and the forthcoming *More Truly and More Strange: 100 Contemporary American Self-Portrait Poems* (Persea, 2020). Her awards include a Guggenheim Fellowship and a Rona Jaffe Award for Emerging Women Writers. Her work has appeared in journals such as *The New Yorker, Poetry, The Kenyon Review, Ploughshares, the Virginia Quarterly Review,* and elsewhere.

Michael Stillman, well-known as founder of Underwood Jazz Society, plays soprano and alto saxophones in venues around the Columbia River Gorge. This follows five decades in academic life — University of Virginia, Harvard, Stanford — studying, teaching, and performing music and literature. His poems and light verse are published widely.

David Trinidad's most recent book of poems is *Swinging on a Star* (Turtle Point Press, 2017). His other books include *Notes on a Past Life* (BlazeVOX [books], 2016) and *Peyton Place: A Haiku Soap Opera* (Turtle Point, 2013). *Punk Rock Is Cool for the End of World: Poems and Notebooks of Ed Smith*, which he edited, was published by Turtle Point in 2019. Trinidad lives in Chicago, where he teaches at Columbia College.

Katrina Vandenberg is the author of two books of poetry, *The Alphabet Not Unlike the World* and *Atlas* (Milkweed Editions). She teaches in the Creative Writing Programs at Hamline University, where she also serves as poetry editor for *Water~Stone Review*.

Michael Waters's recent books include *The Dean of Discipline* (University of Pittsburgh Press, 2018) and *Celestial Joyride* (BOA Editions, 2016), and a coedited anthology, *Reel Verse* (Knopf, 2019). His new book, *Caw*, will appear from BOA in 2020. A 2017 Guggenheim Fellow and recipient of five Pushcart Prizes and fellowships from the National Endowment for the Arts, Fulbright Foundation and NJ State Council on the Arts, Waters teaches at Monmouth University and for the Drew University MFA Program.

Charles Harper Webb's latest books are *Sidebend World* (2018) *Brain Camp* (2015) and *What Things Are Made Of* (2013). He earned a BA in English from Rice University, an MA in English from the University of Washington, and an MFA in professional writing and a PhD in counseling psychology from USC. He teaches at California State University, Long Beach.

Marcus Wicker is the recipient of a Ruth Lilly Fellowship, a Pushcart Prize, *The Missouri Review*'s Miller Audio Prize, as well as fellowships from Cave Canem, and the Fine Arts Work Center. His first collection, *Maybe the Saddest Thing*, a National Poetry Series winner, was a finalist for an NAACP Image Award. Wicker's poems have appeared in *The Nation*, *Poetry*, *American Poetry Review*, *Oxford American*, and *Boston Review*. His second book, *Silencer*, published by Houghton Mifflin Harcourt in 2017, won the Arnold Adoff Poetry Award for New Voices.

David Wojahn's ninth collection of poetry, *For the Scribe*, was published in the Pitt Poetry Series in 2017. He has been a Guggenheim and NEA fellow, and winner of the Academy of American Poets' Lenore Marshall Prize, as well as a named finalist for the Pulitzer Prize for *Interrogation Palace*, his volume of new and selected poems. He teaches at Virginia Commonwealth University, and in the MFA in Writing Program of Vermont College of Fine Arts.

Kevin Young is the author of eleven books of poetry and prose including *Blue Laws: Selected & Uncollected Poems 1995-2015* (2016); *Book of Hours* (2014), a finalist for the Kingsley TuftsAward and winner of the Lenore Marshall Prize for Poetry from the Academy of American Poets; *Ardency: A Chronicle of the Amistad Rebels* (2011); and *Dear Darkness* (2008). His collection *Jelly Roll: a blues* (2003) was a finalist for both the National Book Award and the Los Angeles Times Book Award for Poetry.

Paul Zimmer was the assistant director of the University of Pittsburgh Press and editor of the Pitt Poetry Series from 1967-1978. He directed the University of Georgia Press from 1978-1984, and then the University of Iowa Press from 1984-1994. He is the author of many books of poetry, including *The Great Bird of Love* (1989) and *Crossing to Sunlight* (1996). Zimmer has received various awards and honors for his poetry and prose, including six Pushcart Prizes, two National Endowment for the Arts Literature Fellowships, and a Helen Bullis Memorial Award.

Author Index

Title Index

Musician/Band Index

Acknowledgments/Permissions

I'd like to acknowledge The University of Vermont's Faculty Development Grant for the Arts, which helped make the necessary permissions of this anthology possible. A sabbatical from the English Department also greatly assisted in the creation of this book. Boundless thanks to Neil Shepard for his meticulous and tireless editorial eye, and to Dede Cummings for the attention she paid to all the quirks of poetry in her design. Thanks also to Tamra Higgins for her support and to Pamela Harrison for her editorial eye.

Every effort has been made to trace copyright for the poems included herein. The editor gratefully acknowledges the following permissions:

Kim Addonizio. "Blues for Robert Johnson" and "This Poem Wants to Be a Rock and Roll Song So Bad," from *what is this thing called love: poems* by Kim Addonizio. Copyright 2004 by Kim Addonizio. Used by permission of W.W. Norton & Company, Inc; "When Joe Filisko Plays the Blues," "Cigar Box Banjo" and "Open Mic" from *My Black Angel*. Copyright 2014 by Kim Addonizio. Reprinted by permission of the author.

Boundless thanks to Neil Shepard for his meticulous and tireless editorial eye, and to Dede Cummings for the attention she paid to all the quirks of poetry in her design. Thanks also to Tamra Higgins for her support and to Pamela Harrison for her editorial eye.

Ai. "Archangel" from *Greed* by Ai. Copyright 1993 by Ai. Reprinted by permission of W.W. Norton & Company. Inc.

James Baldwin. "Le sporting-club de Monte Carlo" is collected in *Jimmy's Blues and Other Poems*. Copyright 2014 by the James Baldwin Estate. Published by Beacon Press.

Amiri Baraka. Excerpt from *SOS: Poems 1961-2013* by The Estate of Amiri Baraka. Used by permission of Grove/Atlantic, Inc. Any third party use of this material, outside of this publication, is prohibited.

Tara Betts. "Understanding Tina Turner" from *Arc & Hue*. Copyright 2009 by Tara Betts and reprinted by permission of the author. "Hip Hop Analogies" reprinted by permission of the author. "A Lesson from the Terrordome" from *Break the Habit*. Copyright 2016 by Tara Betts and reprinted by permission of Trio House Press and the author.

Sarah Blake. "Runaway Premiers in Los Angeles on October 18, 2010," "Ha Ha Hum" and "Like the Poems Do" from *Mr. West*. Published by Wesleyan University Press and used by permission of the press.

Adrea Bogle. "Off Minor," from *Brilliant Corners: A Journal of Jazz and Literature*. Reprinted by permission of the author.

Jim Carroll. "8 Fragments for Kurt Cobain" from *Void of Course* by Jim Carroll. Copyright 1998 by Jim Carroll. Used by permission of Viking Books, an imprint of Penguin Publishing Group, a division of Penguin Random House LLC. All rights reserved.

Michael Cirelli. "The Message," "Love Song for Kelis," "Lobster with Ol' Dirty Bastard," "KRS-1 Sleeps at Prospect Park," "When Talib Kweli Gets Expelled from Brooklyn Tech," and "Phife Dawg Awaits a Kidney" are reprinted from *Lobster with Ol' Dirty Bastard*. Copyright 2008 by Michael Cirelli by permission of Hanging Loose Press.

Wanda Coleman. "but, ruby my dear" from *African Sleeping Sickness: Stories & Poems*. Copyright 1990 by Wanda Coleman. Reprinted by permission of David R. Godine, Inc.

Billy Collins. "Man Listening to Disc" from *Sailing Alone Around the Room: New and Selected Poems* by Billy Collins. Copyright 2001 by Billy Collins. Used by permission of Random House, an imprint and division of Penguin Random House LLC. All rights reserved. "The Blues" from *The Art of Drowning*, by Billy Collins, Copyright 1995. Reprinted by permission of the University of Pittsburgh Press.

Kevin Coval. "the cash register in Dr. Dre's head goes bling," "robert van winkle has some tough decisions to make," "the beastie boys cast a video for paul's boutique," "the crossover," and "molemen beat tapes" are from *L-vis Lives!: Racemusic Poems*. Copyright 2011 by Kevin Coval. Reprinted by permission of Haymarket Books.

Stephen Cramer. "Sonnets Ending with a Line by Miles" and "Bone Music" from *Bone Music* (Trio House Press, 2016). Reprinted by permission of the author. "Fight the Power" and "Rising Down" from *From the Hip* (Windridge Books, 2014). Reprinted by permission of the author. "In Bloom" is printed by permission of the author.

Kyle Dargan. "O.P.P." is reprinted by permission of the author.

Toi Derricotte. "Blackbottom" from *Captivity*. Copyright 1998 and reprinted by permission of University of Pittsburgh Press.

Joel Dias-Porter. "Turning the Tables" from *Poetry Magazine*. Copyright 2015 by Joel Dias-Porter. Reprinted by permission of the author.

Mark Doty. "Almost Blue" from *My Alexandria*. Copyright 1993 by Mark Doty and reprinted by permission of the University of Illinois Press.

Rita Dove. "Canary" Copyright 1989 by Rita Dove, "Golden Oldie" Copyright 1995 by Rita Dove, from *Collected Poems: 1974-2004*. Reprinted by permission of W.W. Norton & Company, Inc.

Alysia Nicole Harris. "When I Put My Hands in the Air It's Praise" is printed by permission of the author.

Terrance Hayes. "What It Look Like" from *How to Be Drawn*. Copyright 2015 by Terrance Hayes and reprinted by permission of Penguin Books, an imprint of Penguin Publishing Group, a division of Penguin Random House LLC. All rights reserved; "emcee" from *Hip Logic*. Copyright 2002 by Terrance Hayes and reprinted by permission of Penguin Publishing Group, a division of Penguin Random House LLC. All rights reserved.

Tony Hoagland. "All Along the Watchtower" from *Sweet Ruin,* Copyright 1992 by The Board of Regents of the University of Wisconsin System and reprinted by permission of The University of Wisconsin Press; "Are You Experienced?" from *Donkey Gospel*. Copyright 1998 by Tony Hoagland and reprinted by permission of the Permissions Company, Inc. on behalf of Graywolf Press, Minneapolis, Minnesota, www.graywolfpress.org.

Anna Claire Hodge. "Elegy, Fort Green" is printed by permission of the author.

Chinaka Hodge. "Small Poems for Big" and "2pac couplets" from *Dated Emcees*. Copyright 2016 by Chinaka Hodge and reprinted with the permission of The Permissions Company, Inc., on behalf of City Lights Books, www.citylights.com.

Marie Howe. "Without Music" from *What the Living Do*. Copyright 1997 by Marie Howe, and reprinted by permission of W.W. Norton & Company, Inc.

Langston Hughes. "The Weary Blues," "Jazzonia," "Trumpet Player," and "Song for Billie Holiday" from *The Collected Poems of Langston Hughes*, edited by Arnold Rampersad with David Roessel, Associate Editor. Copyright 1994 by the Estate of Langston Hughes and reprinted by permission of Alfred A. Knopf, an imprint of Knopf Doubleday Publishing Group, a division of Penguin Random House LLC. All rights reserved.

Lynda Hull. "Chiffon," "Ornithology," "Hollywood Jazz" from *Collected Poems*. Copyright 1995 by Lynda Hull and reprinted by permission of The Permissions Company, Inc., on behalf of Graywolf Press, Minneapolis, Minnesota, www.graywolfpress.org. "Lost Fugue for Chet" from Star Ledger. Copyright 1991 by Lynda Hull and reprinted by permission of the University of Iowa Press. All rights reserved.

Angela Jackson. "Billie in Silk" from *Dark Legs and Silk Kisses*. Copyright 1993 by Angela Jackson and reprinted by permission of TriQuarterly Books/Northwestern University Press. All rights reserved.

Major Jackson. "Erie," "Silk City", from *Hoops*. Copyright 2006 by Major Jackson and reprinted by permission of W.W. Norton & Company, Inc.

David Jauss. "Black Orchid"originally appeared in the *Indiana Review*. Copyright 1994 by David Jauss. Reprinted by permission of the author.

Tyehimba Jess. "leadbelly: from sugarland" and "martha promise receives leadbelly, 1935," from *leadbelly*. Copyright 2005 by Tyehimba Jess and reprinted by permission of the author.

William Matthews. Copyright 2004 by Sebastian Matthews and Stanley Plumly and reprinted by permission of Houghton Mifflin Harcourt Publishing Company. All rights reserved.

jessica Care moore. "Poetry Suite for Karriem Riggins" printed by permission of the author.

Stanley Moss. "A Riff for Sidney Bechet" from *A History of Color: New and Selected Poems.* Copyright 2003 by Seven Stories Press and used by permission of the author.

Lisel Mueller. "The Deaf Dancing to Rock" from *Waving from Shore: Poems.* Copyright 1979, 1986, 1987, 1988, 1989 by Lisel Mueller and reprinted by permission of Louisiana State University Press.

Paul Muldoon. "Comeback," "It's Never Too Late for Rock 'n' Roll," and "Dream Team" from *The Word on the Street: Rock Lyrics.* Copyright 2013 by Paul Muldoon and reprinted by permission of Farrar, Straus and Giroux.

John Murillo. "Ode to the Crossfader" and "1989" from *Up Jump the Boogie: Poems.* Copyright 2010 by Cypher Books and reprinted by permission of the author.

Angel Nafis. "Kanye West to Angel Nafis On the Eve of Her Almost Non-Graduation from High School" is printed by permission of the author.

Idra Novey. "The Wailers in Estadio Nacional" from *Rattapallax* no 4. reprinted by permission of the author.

Joyce Carol Oates. "Waiting on Elvis, 1956" from *The Time Traveler* (New York, Dutton). Copyright 1989 by *Ontario Review* and reprinted by permission of the author.

Frank O'Hara. "The Day Lady Died" from *Lunch Poems.* Copyright 1964 by Frank O'Hara and reprinted by permission of The Permissions Company, Inc., on behalf of City Lights Books, www.citylights.com.

Morgan Parker. "Please Wait (Or, There Are More Beautiful Things Than Beyoncé)" from *There Are More Beautiful Things Than Beyoncé.* Copyright 2017 by Morgan Parker and reprinted by permission of the author.

David Rivard. "Cures" from *Torque.* Copyright 1988 by David Rivard and reprinted by permission of the University of Pittsburgh Press.

Patrick Rosal. "B-boy Infinitives" from *Uprock Headspin Scramble and Dive.* Copyright 2003 by Patrick Rosal and reprinted by permission of Persea Books, Inc. (New York); "A Scavenger's Ode to the Turntable" from *Brooklyn Antediluvian.* Copyright 2016 by Patrick Rosal and reprinted with the permission of Persea Books, Inc (New York). All rights reserved.

Muriel Rukeyser. "Bunk Johnson Blowing" from *The Collected Poems of Muriel Rukeyser* Copyright 2005 by Muriel Rukeyser and reprinted by permission of ICM Partners.

Las Vegas, 1976," "Francis Ford Coppola and Anthropologist Interpreter Teaching Gartewienna Tribesmen to Sing "Light My Fire," Philippine Jungle, 1978," and "The Assassination of Lennon as Depicted by then Madame Tussaud Wax Museum, Niagara Falls, Ontario, 1987" from *Mystery Train*. Copyright 1990 by David Wojahn and reprinted by permission of the University of Pittsburgh Press. "Homage to Blind Willie Johnson" from *Interrogation Palace: New and Selected Poems 1982-2004*. Copyright 2011 by David Wojahn and reprinted by permission of the University of Pittsburgh Press. "World Tree" from *World Tree* by David Wojahn, Copyright 2011. Reprinted by permission of University of Pittsburgh Press; "Hey, Joe," from *The Falling Hour*. Copyright 1997 by David Wojahn and reprinted by permission of the University of Pittsburgh Press.

Kevin Young. "Slide Guitar," "Blues," "Disaster Movie Theme Music" from *Jelly Roll: A Blues*. Copyright 2003 by Kevin Young and reprinted by Alfred A. Knopf, an imprint of the Knopf Doubleday Publishing Group, a division of Penguin Random House LLC. All rights reserved; "Expecting" from *Blue Laws: Selected and Uncollected Poems, 1995-2015*. Copyright 2016 by Kevin Young and used by permission of Alfred A. Knopf, an imprint of the Knopf Doubleday Publishing Group, a division of Penguin Random House LLC. All rights reserved.

Paul Zimmer. "But Bird" from *Big Blue Train*. Copyright 1993 by Paul Zimmer; "Zimmer's Last Gig" and "The Duke Ellington Dream" from *Family Reunion*. Copyright 1983 by Paul Zimmer. Reprinted by permission of the author.